T0319061

Cambridge Elements ≡

Elements in Public and Nonprofit Administration
edited by
Andrew Whitford
University of Georgia
Robert Christensen
Brigham Young University

MOTIVATING PUBLIC EMPLOYEES

Marc Esteve
University College London
Christian Schuster
University College London

CAMBRIDGE
UNIVERSITY PRESS

CAMBRIDGE
UNIVERSITY PRESS

University Printing House, Cambridge CB2 8BS, United Kingdom

One Liberty Plaza, 20th Floor, New York, NY 10006, USA

477 Williamstown Road, Port Melbourne, VIC 3207, Australia

314–321, 3rd Floor, Plot 3, Splendor Forum, Jasola District Centre,
New Delhi – 110025, India

79 Anson Road, #06–04/06, Singapore 079906

Cambridge University Press is part of the University of Cambridge.

It furthers the University's mission by disseminating knowledge in the pursuit of
education, learning, and research at the highest international levels of excellence.

www.cambridge.org
Information on this title: www.cambridge.org/9781108459235
DOI: 10.1017/9781108559720

© Marc Esteve and Christian Schuster 2019

First published 2019

A catalogue record for this publication is available from the British Library.

ISBN 978-1-108-45923-5 Paperback
ISSN 2515-4303 (online)
ISSN 2515-429X (print)

Motivating Public Employees

Elements in Public and Nonprofit Administration

DOI: 10.1017/9781108559720
First published online: June 2019

Marc Esteve
University College London & ESADE Business School

Christian Schuster
University College London

Author for correspondence: Marc Esteve, marc.esteve@ucl.ac.uk

Abstract: What motivates public employees to work hard? This Element systematically reviews answers from public administration research. We locate this research in a novel two-dimensional typology which shows that public employees can be motivated for other- and self-interested reasons; and extrinsic (motivated by outcomes) and intrinsic (motivated by work itself) reasons. Public administration research sheds significant light on extrinsic motivators: working hard to help society (public service motivation), one's organization (organizational commitment) and oneself (financial incentives). Future research should focus on hitherto understudied motivators: symbolic rewards and intrinsic motivators, such as enjoyable work tasks, warm glow and relatedness with colleagues. Supplementary material for this Element is available at www.cambridge.org/mpe.

Keywords: Motivation, Intrinsic Motivators, Extrinsic Motivators, Individual Performance, Organizational Commitment

ISBNs: 9781108459235 (PB), 9781108559720 (OC)
ISSNs: 2515-4303 (online), 2515-429X (print)

Contents

1 Motivation as the Holy Grail of Public Management

The lazy bureaucrat problem is ancient, as old as bureaucracy itself.
The Guardian, 2010

This is what you get from lousy government bureaucrats ... loyalty to each other, selflessness in the line of duty, and dedication to protect the public they serve.
Federal prison doctor held hostage during a riot, cited in DiIulio (1994)

A motivated workforce is a foundation of organizational effectiveness. The performance of employees depends on their motivation to work hard towards organizational purposes; and their retention depends on their motivation to remain within the organization (Pinder, 2008). A de-motivated workforce is thus costly to organizations. The US army, for instance, needs to spend the equivalent of a large truck to replace a trained reservist who quits – not speaking of the disruptions to working relationships, lost corporate knowledge and setbacks to projects which additionally come from staff departures (Thomas, 2000).

While motivating employees has thus been a perennial challenge for managers, it has been rarely as important as today. Changes in the very nature of work put a greater premium on it. With technological innovation alongside demands for greater customization of products and services, many routine, low-skilled tasks – which could be solved through following rules – are increasingly automatized or outsourced offshore. By contrast, high-skilled, heuristic tasks – non-routine work which requires self-direction and creativity – claim an increasing share of work (McKinsey, 2017). At the same time, better management information systems have enabled flatter hierarchies in organizations, which cut costs and shift greater decision-making power from now-redundant middle managers to frontline employees – who are called on to adapt to customer needs, simplify procedures and innovate. In conjunction, these shifts implicate that successful organizations increasingly require self-motivated and committed employees to undertake self-directed tasks, adapt to client needs, and push for innovation on the front line (Pink, 2009).

Arguably, this holds nowhere more so than in public sector organizations. As their private sector counterparts, governments see an increasing shift towards higher-skilled, non-routine jobs (DiIulio, 2014). At the same time, they have also seen a historic decline in citizen trust. Motivated employees who deliver effective services to the public are thus central to regain – or at least retain the remaining – citizen trust in government (OECD, 2016). Motivating staff has, however, arguably rarely been more challenging for public managers than today. Governments in OECD countries in particular face austerity pressures which have curbed pay and enhanced workloads – and, unsurprisingly,

de-motivated staff (Esteve, Schuster, Albareda & Losada, 2017). This
has been paralleled by the rise of populist governments with frequent anti-
bureaucracy and anti-state rhetoric. Understandably, this bureaucracy-
bashing is de-motivating bureaucrats (Jahan & Shahan, 2012).

Motivating staff is thus central. Despite its centrality, however, organizations – public and private alike – are often not successful at motivating
staff. A recent study, for instance, suggests that being sick is the only activity
during which individuals are, on average, less happy than at work (Bryson &
MacKerron, 2017); and Gallup surveys suggest that 85 per cent of employees
worldwide are not engaged in their jobs (Gallup, 2017). Work motivation in the
public sector fares, according to popular stereotypes, even worse. Public
employees have a reputation for being lethargic and lazy (Wilson, 1989,
p. xviiii); and, though this is contested in the literature, some empirical studies
suggests that they, in fact, *are* lazier than their private sector counterparts (e.g.
Dur & Zoutenbier, 2015). As the second epigraph underscores, however, the
public sector also abounds with employees who go above and beyond their call
of duty and 'care like you wouldn't believe' (Brehm & Gates, 1997; Dilulio,
1994, p. 287).

This puts a premium on understanding why some employees are motivated
to work hard yet others are not – and what organizations can do to maximize
workforce motivation.[1] The literature on this conundrum is huge. Roughly
65,000 articles or books published from 1950 to 2008 contain the word
"motivation" in their title or abstract (Landy & Conte, 2010, p. 360). And work
motivation has been the subject of both dedicated textbooks (e.g. Latham, 2012;
Pinder, 2008) and popular bestsellers (e.g. Pink, 2009).

Yet, why some *public* employees are motivated to work hard yet others are
not – and what *public* organizations can do to maximize workforce motivation –
has, to our knowledge, not seen a systematic review or book-length treatment.[2]

---

[1] In the remainder of this Element, we take for granted that maximizing work motivation is
desirable. While this is more often true than not, a literature on burn-out and organizational
addiction reminds us that this need not always be the case. Highly pro-socially motivated
employees who do not perceive a societal impact of their work, for instance, have been found
to be more likely to burn out (e.g. van Loon, Vandenabeele & Leisink, 2015). Moreover,
excessive organizational commitment can be 'addictive', with people losing 'touch with other
aspects of their lives and gradually [giving] up what they knew, felt and believed' (Schaef &
Fassel, 1988, p. 119). Such excessive commitment in turn may lead to a greater propensity to
engage in illegal or immoral activities for the organization (Wiener, 1982). In other words,
excessive organizational commitment may have problematic implications for the direction of
work effort from a public interest perspective. The remainder of this Element should be read
with this caveat in mind.

[2] The descriptive reviews in Wright (2001), Le Grand (2003) and Perry, Mesch & Paarlberg (2006)
are partial exceptions.

Public sector contexts, however, are unique in the motivational opportunities and challenges they present.[3]

Three challenges stand out. First, public sectors are typically characterized by constraints on performance incentives. Though these have been targets of reform in many countries, career civil services coupled with public sector union pressure for collective pay frequently implicate lifelong job contracts with protections against dismissals and pay tied to seniority – rather than performance – in the public sector. As a result, managers are deprived of significant material incentives to motivate staff. Instead, such systems 'insure' public employees against adverse consequences from shirking and poor work effort on the job. Consequently, civil service systems may foster what rational choice scholars term 'adverse selection': the attraction of staff who prefer organizations in which benefits (such as pay) are unrelated to effort – i.e. the attraction of staff who prefer putting in less effort (Delfgaauw & Dur, 2008; Wilson, 1989). Second, public sectors – and civil services in particular – are often characterized by a greater predominance of administrative jobs and detailed, standardized terms of reference and operating procedures (Perry & Porter, 1982). As detailed in Section 2, such jobs significantly reduce the intrinsic motivating potential of jobs. Third, the declining esteem of government complicates attracting, retaining and cultivating motivated staff (Jahan & Shahan, 2012). Lastly, political contestation over what public sector organizations are to achieve and the inherent difficulty of measuring public sector goals translate into objectives which are often vague, multiple, conflicting and unstable (Moore, 1996). This complicates goal setting to motivate staff (see Section 3 for further detail). Difficulties in measuring what public organizations and employees achieve, coupled with a need for democratic accountability, furthermore often contribute to greater procedural constraints on public employee action (Perry & Rainey, 1988; Wright, 2001). Public sector managers thus often have more tools to prevent employees from doing something wrong than to motivate them to do something right (Behn, 1995). Motivating employees is thus both uniquely challenging and uniquely difficult in the public sector.

It is, however, also, in some ways, uniquely possible. Most prominently, public sector organizations attract staff who have a sense of calling and are motivated to serve society and the public interest (Besley & Ghatak, 2018; Perry & Wise, 1990). Public managers thus have greater opportunities to motivate staff through pro-social – or public service – motivators. Moreover,

---

[3] While these unique challenges and opportunities for workforce motivation in the public sector are widely accepted in the public administration literature, there is only limited research which has established them empirically (cf. Wright, 2001).

lifelong employment offers greater opportunities for managers to develop an *esprit de corps* in staff: a feeling of pride and loyalty among staff towards their peer group and a commitment to the organization more generally (Dilulio, 1994; Wilson, 1989). Career job contracts also enable managers to motivate through long-term career – rather than short-term pay – incentives. Lastly, the unique job content in many civil service positions in particular – revolving around policy and politics – amplifies opportunities for public managers to make jobs inherently interesting and enjoyable and thus motivates staff intrinsically.

These unique challenges and opportunities, of course, do not imply that the insights from the large literature on work motivation in the private sector have no bearing on the public sector. They do, however, imply that applying and adapting these theories requires consideration of the unique public sector context (cf. Perry, Mesch & Paarlberg, 2006; Wright, 2001). As a result, understanding how to motivate public employees is a central research endeavour and one of the 'big questions' in public management (Behn, 1995, p. 313).

Nonetheless and somewhat curiously, no systematic and comprehensive review of public administration research on why some public employees are motivated to work hard – yet others are not – exists to date. This Element addresses this gap. It develops a holistic typology to understand the range of motivators in the public sector and takes stock of what we can learn from public administration research about these motivators and management practices to enhance them. In comparing these findings with insights about work motivation from the management, economics and psychology literature, this Element also sheds light on what public administration scholars have focused on in the study of work motivation in the public sector – and what they have neglected or missed.

Scholars of work motivation in the public sector might, of course, raise an immediate objection to this endeavour. Among topics in public administration, research on public service motivation (PSM) – the 'beliefs, value and attitudes that go beyond self-interest and organisational interest, that concern the interest of a larger political entity and that motivate individuals to act accordingly whenever appropriate' (Vandenabeele, 2007, p. 549) – 'stands out by [its] sheer numbers', with more than fifty studies published every year in the last years (Ritz, Brewer & Neumann, 2016; Rainey & Steinbauer, 1999, p. 20); and this research has, in fact, seen a number of recent literature reviews (e.g. Christensen, Paarlberg & Perry, 2017; Prebble, 2016; Ritz et al., 2016) and book-length treatments (Perry & Hondeghem, 2008). The attention PSM has received need not surprise. PSM research was originally motivated by and provided a powerful antidote to rational-choice critiques of bureaucracy

(Perry & Wise, 1990). These economic critiques were premised on assumptions of public servants as self-interested utility maximizers and provided (part of) the intellectual foundation for the introduction of performance incentive systems and downsizing in government (Niskanen, 1968; Osborne, 1993). PSM scholars were keenly concerned that such practices would undermine – or crowd out – a public service ethic in government (Perry & Wise, 1990). Judging by the sheer number of works on PSM and the greater attention paid to pro-social motivation of public servants in the economics literature – where the rational-choice critique of bureaucracy had largely originated (see e.g. Besley & Ghatak, 2018) – PSM research has been successful at shifting attention towards behaviours that help others, rather than self-interested behaviour, in public service.

PSM and self-interested economic incentives, however, are far from the only sources of work motivation in the public sector. As we evidence in this Element, the attention to PSM, incentives and related theories has not been paralleled by equally comprehensive research programmes on other potential sources of work motivation in the public sector. As a result, public administration scholarship to date falls short of providing a holistic understanding of the determinants of work motivation in the public sector.

This Element seeks to address this shortcoming by providing such a holistic analysis. In doing so, it seeks to encourage scholars to pay greater attention to sources of work motivation in the public sector beyond serving the public and responding to economic incentives and goals, while providing guidance to practitioners and students who seek to understand how to motivate public employees.

We do so in three steps. First, in Section 2, we develop a holistic typology to understand the sources of work motivation in the public sector. Conceptualizing work motivation as both the direction and intensity of effort, we integrate several theoretical perspectives – including self-determination theory, principal-agent theory, social identity theory, pro-social motivation theory and organizational commitment theory – to develop a two-dimensional typology of motivators in the public sector. Our typology underscores that public employees can be motivated for self- or other-regarding reasons and, at the same time, for intrinsic reasons (motivated by work activity itself) or extrinsic reasons (because work activity leads to a separable outcome employees value). We show that six core motivators can be located in this two-dimensional space. These comprise three extrinsic motivators – pro-social motivation (working to help attain outcomes for society), organizational and group commitment (working to help attain outcomes for an organization or group one identifies with) and incentives (working to help attain self-interested goals) – and three intrinsic motivators: enjoyment (finding work tasks themselves pleasurable); relatedness (finding work pleasurable due to connections and interactions with colleagues) and warm glow (finding it pleasurable to help others with work). We, further, show how insights from other theoretical lenses – including equity theory and needs-based theories – can be integrated into our typology to expand its explanatory prowess. Lastly, we delineate the utility of our typology for practice by deriving several lessons for how to motivate public employees in practice based on it.

In Section 3, we take this typology to public administration research and systematically review and assess what can be learned from public administration studies about the determinants of our six motivators in the public sector and management practices to foment them. Based on a systematic literature review, we first assess what and how public administration has researched work motivation in the public sector – and what it has neglected. We find that research to date has focused overwhelmingly on public sector work motivation in the West – and, in particular, the United States. We know much less about what motivates public employees in developing countries. What we do know, moreover, comes principally from partial correlations in observational studies – a problematic basis for *causal* inferences about what motivates public employees; this is made worse by the lack of a generally accepted and validated scale to measure work motivation in the public sector. Instead, different studies conceptualize and measure public employee work motivation in different ways. Inconsistent findings about what motivates public employees might thus simply stem from different ways of conceptualizing or measuring public sector work motivation. With this caveat in mind, our review underscores that motivating public employees is invariably complex: individual-, job-, management- and organizational-level factors all interact to shape whether public employees are motivated to work hard. There are thus no silver bullets for motivating public employees. We also find that public administration has paid relatively more attention to determinants of PSM, organizational commitment and financial incentives. It has paid less attention to other motivators: non-pecuniary incentives, task enjoyment, relatedness and warm glow.

In the final section, we move from determinants of public employee work motivation to lessons for practice. How can public managers and organizations motivate their employees? We first detail the most frequently mentioned lessons in public administration research. Subsequently, we turn to insights from other disciplines – economics, psychology and management studies – for lessons about motivators which public administration research neglects: non-pecuniary self-interested incentives, task enjoyment, relatedness and warm glow. Future research in public administration would do well to consider these motivators to enable a more holistic understanding of public sector work motivation. Public sector practitioners would stand to benefit.

2 Work Motivation in the Public Sector: a Typology

Why are some public employees more motivated at work than others? This section provides a two-dimensional typology to classify and understand sources of work motivation in the public sector. It argues that these can be understood through a two-dimensional typology – from self- to other-regarding and from intrinsic to extrinsic sources of motivation; and that six sources of public sector work motivation can be differentiated based on this typology; three extrinsic sources: pro-social motivation; organizational/group identification and incentives; and three intrinsic sources: enjoyment, related-ness and warm glow. To contextualize typology development, the section starts by conceptualizing work motivation.

2.1 What Is Work Motivation?

Motivation has its origins in Latin (*movere*), where it means 'to move'. To be motivated then is to be moved to do something (Ryan & Deci, 2000b). In other – and less colloquial – words, motivation is the psychological process that leads individuals to behave in a particular way (Vroom, 1964). At work, motivation is often equated with the 'the degree to which an individual wants and tries hard to do well at a particular task or job' (Mitchell, 1982, p. 81).[4]

Work motivation is thus an individual phenomenon. As individuals are unique – they have different needs, goals and values, for instance – they will be motivated by different factors (Mitchell, 1982). Any valid theory or typology of work motivation thus needs to account for this uniqueness of individuals in the workplace: different individuals are motivated by different factors. Our typology in the next section takes this into account.

The definition above also underscores that work motivation is typically described as *intentional* – that is, employees may *choose* whether to put effort into a particular task or job (Mitchell, 1982). In that sense, motivating employees implies *instilling* motivation inside employees.

Lastly – and perhaps most importantly – motivation is a multidimensional concept. It is typically conceptualized to comprise not only the *intensity* of action (cognitive effort and/or physical force of action) that is colloquially

---

[4] As a caveat, there is no singular, widely accepted definition of motivation. Kleinginna and Kleinginna (1981), for instance, find 140 different definitions of motivation.

typically associated with it; but also the *persistence* of behaviour and its *direction*: 'motivation [has been] frequently described in work settings by referring to what a person does (direction), how hard a person works (intensity), and how long a person works (persistence)' (Kanfer, 1990, p. 78). Other conceptualizations often make similar reference to these three components but with varying terminology. Mitchell (1982, p. 81), for instance, defines it as 'those psychological processes that cause the arousal, direction, and persistence of voluntary actions that are goal directed' – thus equating intensity with arousal. Similarly, Perry and Porter (1982, p. 89) define motivation as 'that which energizes, directs and sustains behaviour' – thus equating intensity to that which 'energizes' and persistence to that which 'sustains' behaviour. Of these three components, however, persistence is often given less weight when explaining individual action (Mitchell, 1982). This is in part because persistence can be understood as the reaffirmation of the initial choice of action (March & Simon, 1958).

For our purposes, then, we can collapse the conceptualization of work motivation in the public sector into two dimensions: the amount of effort employees are willing to invest into their work (intensity of work effort); and the direction of their effort – that is, what objectives or purposes public employees are working towards with their effort (direction of work effort).

Any holistic typology or theory of work motivation in the public sector thus needs to be able to account for both the intensity and direction of work effort in the public sector. In addition, as already noted, it needs to account for the uniqueness of work motivation – different individuals are motivated by different factors – in the workplace. The typology we develop in the next section takes on this task.

2.2 Sources of Work Motivation: a Typology

Why are some employees more motivated at work than others? A vast literature and disparate set of theories have sought to respond to this conundrum (Pinder, 2008). Our strategy for typology-building in this section thus loosely follows Allison's (1969): relying on a single theory – of many – leaves important parts of reality unexplored. By contrast, integrating multiple theoretical lenses enables a more comprehensive understanding. With this in mind, this section synthesizes a range of prior theories – including self-determination theory, principal-agent theory, expectancy theory, pro-social motivation theory and organizational commitment theory – to develop a two-dimensional typology to holistically explain sources of work motivation in the public sector. As illustrated in Figure 1, we will argue that, the complexity of work motivation notwithstanding, these motivational sources can be helpfully understood

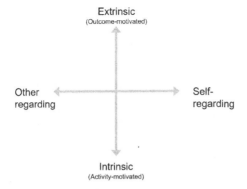

Figure 1 A two-dimensional typology of work motivation

alongside two dimensions: extrinsic versus intrinsic motivators; and others-versus self-interested motivators.

We first develop the y-axis of the typology: intrinsic versus extrinsic sources of work motivation. We do so by drawing principally on self-determination theory (SDT) (Ryan & Deci, 2000a). Subsequently, we develop the x-axis of the typology: others- versus self-regarding sources of motivation. This axis of our typology has been at the centre of public administration debates around public service motivation versus rational choice–inspired performance incentives. We build on these debates and a set of related theories of work motivation in developing this dimension and show that it can help understand both the intensity and direction of work effort of public servants.

With the two dimensions clarified, Section 2.3 goes on to discuss and locate six sources of work motivation for public servants – and employees more generally – in our two-dimensional space: pro-social motivation, organizational and group commitment, incentives, enjoyment, relatedness and warm glow. We will argue that each of them can motivate public servants to work hard and that, in conjunction, they provide a holistic insight into the sources of work motivation in the public sector.

2.2.1 Extrinsic versus Intrinsic Motivators

Our y-axis underscores that public employees can be motivated by both extrinsic and intrinsic motivators. The terms 'intrinsic' and 'extrinsic' have different meanings in different theories of work motivation (see Section 2.3). Many of these theories come with built-in constraining assumptions about what motivates employees. Frey and Osterloh (2002, p. 36), for instance, argue that 'employees may work hard for one of two reasons: because they are interested in the work itself (intrinsic motivation) or because they are being paid (extrinsic motivation)'. Yet employees may, of course, be motivated for other reasons, including the opportunity to serve society (Perry & Wise, 1990). For a more holistic typology of sources of work motivation, we thus draw in our conceptualization of 'intrinsic' and 'extrinsic' motivators on our y-axis principally on self-determination theory (SDT) (Deci & Ryan, 1985; Ryan & Deci, 2000a). SDT, further, offers the validity advantage of having seen a range of empirical studies in support of the theory (e.g. Deci, Eghrari, Patrick & Leone, 1994; Deci, Koestner & Ryan, 1999).

In SDT, intrinsic motivation 'is defined as the doing of an activity for its inherent satisfactions rather than for some separable consequences' (Ryan & Deci, 2000a, p. 56). In other words, intrinsic motivation 'refers to doing something because it is inherently interesting or enjoyable'. (Ryan & Deci, 2000a, p. 55) If all behaviour is construed as being motivated by rewards – as operant theory stipulates (Skinner & Burrhus, 1953) – the reward for intrinsically motivated activities lies in the activity itself. Intrinsic motivation thus exists both within individuals and also, in another sense, in the relation between individuals and tasks. It is also, fundamentally, an emotional source of motivation (Thomas, 2000). As we detail in Section 2.3, a range of factors – challenge, feelings of competence, a sense of autonomy and others – can trigger intrinsic motivation.

By contrast, extrinsic motivation 'pertains whenever an activity is done in order to attain some separable outcome' (Ryan & Deci, 2000a, p. 60). In other words, extrinsically motivated activities are undertaken for their instrumental value: to achieve outcomes an employee values. The outcomes which an employee values and is motivated to achieve can have more external or more internalized origins. At the one extreme – in what SDT calls 'external regulation' – they stem from external demands or externally imposed reward contingencies (Ryan & Deci, 2000a, p. 61). Activities solely undertaken to avoid sanctions from management or to obtain a performance bonus, for instance, would be understood as externally regulated. At the other extreme – in what SDT calls 'integrated regulation' – however, employees may also be motivated to attain outcomes because they have internalized and identify with the importance of attaining them. In other words, they are motivated as they are personally committed to the outcomes, which have inward meaning and worth to them and are congruent with their sense of self and values (Deci & Ryan, 1985; Ryan & Deci, 2000a).[5] Early parental and religious socialization, for instance, may internalize public service values in

---

[5] In between these two extremes, SDT stipulates two further forms of extrinsic motivation. 'Identified regulation' is similar to 'integrated regulation' in that individuals consciously value activities and self-endorse goals. However, identified regulations are not fully

individuals, which leads them to value – and be motivated to work towards – better outcomes for society (Perry, 1997). While such activities are still extrinsically motivated by the outcomes they enable employees to achieve, they are more volitional – or *self-determined* – than externally regulated activities.

In short, public employees may be motivated for intrinsic (by the activity itself) or extrinsic (to attain outcomes they value) reasons. Extrinsic motivators may both be externally imposed by managers or organizations and outcomes which public employees internally identify with and self-endorse.[6] These motivators are, of course, not mutually exclusive. An activity might be motivating to public employees as it is inherently enjoyable, as its attainment enables the employee to attain an externally imposed performance target and as, at the same time, the employee self-endorses and values the outcome (e.g. for society) of the activity. We will return to the motivating potential of combining multiple sources of motivation in Section 2.4.

2.2.2 Other- versus Self-Regarding Sources of Motivation

In standard economic theory, individuals are often described as a *homo economicus*: individuals who seek to maximize their own self-interest (Shepsle, 2010). This self-interest can comprise a wide variety of elements – such as wealth, power, fame, pleasure, health or personal development. Economic (rational choice) theories of bureaucracy extend the *homo economicus* to the public sector. They assume public servants are motivated by self-interest (Niskanen, 1968). Le Grand (2003) prominently labelled such public employees *knaves*. They are motivated to work if they perceive that the self-interested benefits they derive from doing so outweigh the costs. New Public Management (NPM)-inspired approaches to workforce motivation – such as performance

---

assimilated to the self, including by 'bringing them into congruence with one's other values and needs' (Ryan & Deci, 2000a, p. 62). 'Introjected regulation' in turn is one step closer to 'external regulation'. (Ryan & Deci, 2000a, p. 62) Individuals are motivated to act under pressure to avoid anxiety or guilt or to enhance or maintain their self-esteem or sense of worth (ego enhancement). While these differences are helpful to disentangle individual motivators, for our more general typology it suffices to note that a distinction can be made between intrinsic and extrinsic motivation as well as between more external and more self-determined extrinsic motivators.

[6] As a theory – rather than mere typology – SDT goes one step further. It argues that humans are fundamentally motivated by self-determination; that they experience externally regulated extrinsic motivators as 'controlled or alienated'; and that external regulation is thus an 'impoverished form of motivation' (Ryan & Deci, 2000a, p. 55 & p. 61). Our typology, by contrast, does not rest on assumptions of superiority of one form of motivation or another. As aforementioned, individuals are unique and motivated by different factors. The y-axis of our typology underscores that these can be understood along an extrinsic–intrinsic continuum.

pay – directly build on this *homo economicus* motivation. It represents one extreme on our 'other versus self-regarding' x-axis.

At the other extreme, public employees may be motivated by '"other-directed" activities, that is, activities which benefit others and which do not positively affect their own material welfare' (Le Grand, 2003, pp. 27–28). Social psychologists frequently use terms such as 'altruistic' or 'pro-social' to refer to such motivation (e.g. Grant, 2008). In public administration research, as further detailed in Section 2.3.3, this form of motivation is commonly referred to as public service motivation (Perry, Hondeghem & Wise, 2010) – though, as will be noted, other-regarding behaviour need not focus on or be motivated by concerns for society or the public as a whole. Le Grand (2003) terms such public employees 'knights'. They are 'motivated to help others for no private reward, and indeed ... may undertake such activities to the detriment of their own private interests' (Le Grand, 2003, p. 27).[7]

Importantly, 'other-' and 'self-regarding' motivators can be understood to lie on a continuum – rather than representing a dichotomy. This holds in two senses. First, individuals rarely approximate 'pure' knights or knaves. Rather, they are frequently motivated by self-interested concerns in some contexts yet other-regarding concerns in others (Le Grand, 2003). Second, 'other-regarding' behaviour need not be motivated by benefiting society as a whole. Rather, it can be motivated by identification with – and benefits for – smaller groups within society. In the narrowest sense, altruistic behaviour towards family and kin is other-regarding behaviour and, in part, genetically motivated (Dawkins, 1989). More usefully for our purposes – and as further detailed in the next section – other-regarding behaviour may also be motivated by a concern for (non-kin) broader social groups with whom individuals identify: their team at work; the organization they work for; their profession; or the political party they are a member of, for instance.

In short, then, our two-dimensional typology suggests that public employees may be motivated at work because of self-interest or other-regarding factors; and, concurrently, because of intrinsic or extrinsic reasons.

With work motivation, we thereby, as noted, refer to the intensity *and* direction of work effort. Our typology provides insights into both. We may, in particular, expect that public employees motivated by self-interest will direct their work effort towards furthering this self-interest; whether such effort also furthers organizational or societal interests will hinge upon alignment between personal, organizational and societal goals. By contrast, public employees

---

[7] Self-interested individuals may, of course, still engage in other-regarding activities, albeit only if – and this is their original source of motivation – they thereby further their own self-interest.

motivated by other-regarding concerns will direct their effort towards benefiting others. In this instance, societal goals are furthered if public employees either identify with society as a whole or with a narrower group within society whose goals are aligned with societal goals.

Sources of work motivation on the 'other' versus 'self-regarding' dimension may thus shape both the intensity and direction of work effort. As we discuss further in Section 2.5, this implicates that different sources of work motivation may crowd each other out. However, motivators along our two dimensions need not necessarily be in conflict. Public employees may be motivated at work because their work is intrinsically enjoyable *and* because their work outcomes further their own self-interested goals *as well as* the goals of an organization they identify with *and* the welfare of society at large.

Public managers seeking to motivate employees thus need to understand in more depth each of these sources of work motivation. We discuss them next.

2.3 Applying the Typology: Work Motivators in the Public Sector

With our two-dimensional typology, we can locate six motivators in the public sector: three extrinsic motivators – pro-social motivation, group/organization identification and incentives; and three intrinsic motivators – enjoyment, relatedness and warm glow (Figure 2). The advantage of our holistic typology – relative to one-dimensional intrinsic versus extrinsic (Ryan & Deci, 2000a) or egoist versus altruist (Le Grand, 2003) distinctions – lies in being able to identify and distinguish these motivators more clearly by their underlying source of motivation.

2.3.1 Incentives

In our typology, incentives are self-regarding extrinsic motivators. In other words, incentivized public employees work hard because doing so enables them to attain outcomes which are in their self-interest.[8] Of our six motivators, the study of incentives first rose to prominence. From the nineteenth century, studies assessed how subjects respond to stimuli, most prominently encapsulated in Pavlov's dog studies. Scholars also started experimenting with how various types of rewards and punishments fomented or curbed performance in animals (in aptly titled articles such as Crespi's (1942) 'Quantitative Variation

---

[8] We use 'incentives' here in its narrower, colloquial 'self-interest' sense. Of course, 'other-regarding' extrinsically motivated behaviour can also be conceptualized as incentivized. Pro-socially motivated employees are, for instance, in a sense pro-socially incentivized to work hard to attain outcomes valued by society (Besley & Ghatak, 2018).

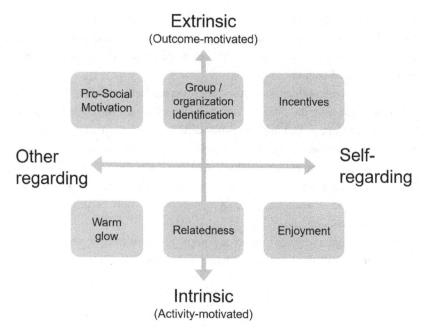

Figure 2 Work motivators in the public sector

of Incentive and Performance in the White Rat'). They generally found support for the notion that incentives motivate behaviour. Numerous theories of motivation have extended this finding to individuals and employees.

Vroom's (1964) expectancy theory argued that employees work hard when they believe that doing so results in a desired outcome. This belief in turn materializes if employees believe that exerting effort will lead to good performance (expectancy); that good performance will be rewarded (instrumentality); and that the reward offered will be of value to the employee (valence). In other words, incentives only incentivize employees where they value the reward and believe that they can *and* will obtain it by putting in effort. Of course, rewards can vary in type. Skinner and Burrhus's (1953) operant condition theory, for instance, argued that behaviour can be shaped by positive reinforcement (providing a reward to reinforce positive behaviour); negative reinforcement (withholding punishment to reinforce positive behaviour); operant extinction (withholding a reward to change negative behaviour); and punishment (punishing to change negative behaviour).

In the public sector, incentives as motivators took centre stage in research with the application of economic (rational choice) theory to bureaucracy. In these theories, bureaucracies are argued to consist of chains of principal-agent relations. Principals (managers) seek to motivate agents (employees) to work hard. To ensure agents work hard, principals need to monitor agent actions and incentivize agents to work hard, through rewards and sanctions. Yet, principals cannot perfectly monitor what agents are doing on their job (information asymmetry), nor – due to strong job protections in many civil services – can they sanction poor work effort through dismissals. Agents thus face incentives to pursue self-interested goals (including prioritizing leisure over work) – unless, of course, principals incentivize them to pursue the principals' goals (and work hard). Such incentives can – in Niskanen's (1968) classic bureaucratic utility function, for instance – include greater budgets, salaries, power, reputation and office perquisites. New Public Management (NPM)-inspired approaches to public employee motivation took this assumption that self-interest motivates public employee behaviour to practice. They tie rewards (pay for performance) and punishments (dismissals) to employee performance to motivate work effort (Osborne, 1993). Roughly two-thirds of OECD public sectors have either implemented or are developing performance pay, for instance (OECD, 2005).

The set of incentives available to managers, however, is of course broader than those typically considered in NPM reforms. Scholars have developed a range of typologies to classify them more holistically (e.g. Barnard, 1968; Clark & Wilson, 1961). In these classifications, incentives include both material inducements or 'tangible rewards' – such as pay, promotion opportunities, maintaining employment, fringe benefits, tax reductions, gifts and physical conditions at work; and non-material, intangible incentives – such as status and prestige, skill development, power and self-esteem (e.g. through praise and recognition). Furthermore, one can differentiate short-term incentives (such as performance bonuses) and long-term incentives (such as better career advancement prospects or long-term skill development) which may motivate staff, and one can also differentiate between incentives for individuals or larger groups, such as teams.

Which of these tangible and intangible incentives effectively motivate staff will, in line with expectancy theory, hinge upon what type of rewards (or lack of sanctions) employees value. In Section 3, we will assess whether, notwithstanding this observation, public administration research provides any general lessons about the general efficacy of different incentives.

2.3.2 Intrinsic Motivators: Enjoyment, Relatedness and Warm Glow

While scholars discovered the power of incentives through experiments with mice and rats, rhesus monkeys provided the foundational insights for research on intrinsic motivation. In experiments, they solved puzzles without given any incentive to do so. They performed because they enjoyed solving puzzles: the 'joy of the task was its own reward' (Pink, 2009, p. 3). In other words, they were motivated by task enjoyment – which sits on the bottom right corner of our typology. Public employees motivated by enjoyment work hard for self-regarding intrinsic reasons: because the work tasks provide them with enjoyment.

Several theories explain why some jobs are more intrinsically enjoyable than others. Hackman and Oldham's job characteristics theory posits that five task characteristics – task identity, task significance, skill variety, autonomy and feedback – shape the intrinsic motivating potential of a job (Hackman, 1980). In other words, public employees are argued to find their jobs more enjoyable if it enables them to use a greater variety of skills (skill variety); if they can see the end result of their work (task identity); if they have a sense that their work is important to others inside or outside the organization (task significance); if they have autonomy – and thus independence and control – to complete the task (autonomy); and if they get feedback about how well they are doing. With these job characteristics in place, employees feel responsible for work outcomes, find them meaningful and know about results – and are thus more intrinsically motivated to work.

Cognitive evaluation theory emphasizes a slightly different set of factors and psychological processes (Deci & Ryan, 1985). It argues that employees are intrinsically motivated when work provides them with, among others, feelings of competence, autonomy and interest. A sense of competence – a human need stemming from a desire to master and control one's environment – can come, for instance, from optimally challenging work and positive feedback; a sense of autonomy – a human need to have a free will and be one's own causal agent – from the opportunity to self-direct work (rather than, for instance, work because of directives or competition pressure); and a sense of interest from activities that have novelty, challenge or aesthetic appeal to employees. Other, overlapping typologies look to, among others, mastery and learning, as well as purpose and autonomy, as being key to intrinsic motivation (Pink, 2009).

While these theories diverge in underlying psychological processes, they do point to an overlapping set of factors which are theorized to make work intrinsically enjoyable: novel, interesting tasks; challenges and a sense of accomplishment and competence; learning, mastery and the use of a variety of skills; autonomy and self-direction of work; seeing the results and getting feedback on one's work; and a sense of purpose and significance of one's work. The integration of multiple intrinsic motivators can lead to what Csikszentmihayli (1975) calls flow experiences: undivided attention towards a task for the sole purpose of task accomplishment.

In the public sector, the prevalence of administrative jobs leads some scholars to the opposite concern: routineness rather than novelty, unclear goals rather than clear task identity and significance, and procedural constraints rather than autonomy and the lack of challenge may all intrinsically de-motivate staff (Buelens & Van den Broeck, 2007). At the same time, however, public sector jobs may also permit participation in public policy formulation, which can be 'exciting, dramatic' and purposeful (Perry & Wise, 1990, p. 368). Public sectors jobs thus certainly *can* be intrinsically enjoyable.

In our typology, intrinsic motivators need not be solely self-regarding. In fact, cognitive evaluation theory itself argues that intrinsic motivation also depends on a sense of relatedness to others at work – a desire to feel emotionally connected to and care for others. High-quality relationships and interactions with others at work can create this sense of relatedness and thus intrinsically motivate staff (Deci & Ryan, 1985). Other theories draw on related concepts, such as affiliation motivation. Affiliation motivation includes, among others, the 'positive affect or stimulation associated with interpersonal closeness and communion ... and the reduction of negative affect [specifically fear and stress] through social contact' (Hill, 1987; cited in Pinder, 2008, p. 173). Relatedness might matter as a motivator in the public sector in particular: there is some evidence that public employees care, relative to private sector employees, especially about positive working relationships with others (see, e.g., Posner & Schmidt, 1996).

Intrinsic, other-regarding motivation may, however, go beyond the narrow group of colleagues employees engage with and relate to at work. Employees might also feel good about helping their organization and society at large with their work – that is, they derive intrinsic motivation from a sense of helping others over and above the pro-social outcomes they attain with their work. This pleasure of making a difference for others is often termed 'warm glow' (Andreoni, 1990; Besley & Ghatak, 2018). In our typology, it is thus located in the bottom left quadrant, as an other-regarding intrinsic motivator.

2.3.3 Pro-social Motivation

Juxtaposed to warm glow, pro-social motivation sits on the top left corner of our typology as an extrinsic, other-regarding motivator. Pro-socially motivated employees are motivated to work hard because of the positive outcomes their work attains for society. Helping others may, of course, motivate public employees intrinsically and extrinsically at the same time: they may enjoy doing so (warm glow) *and* value the outcomes their work attains for society (pro-social motivation).

Under different umbrella terms – such as a public service spirit or public service ethic – pro-social motivation was central to motivational accounts in classic public administration works (e.g. Weber, 1978). As a counter-narrative to economic theories of bureaucracy and the introduction of NPM-style performance incentives, interest in pro-social motivation in public administration has resurged since the 1990s under the public service motivation (PSM) concept (Perry & Wise, 1990). PSM was initially conceptualized to capture a range of rational, affective and normative motivational factors which distinguish the public sector, with Perry and Wise (1990, p. 368) defining PSM as 'an individual's predisposition to respond to motives grounded primarily or uniquely in public institutions and organizations'. At its core, PSM referred to the motives of individuals to display behaviours they believe will promote the public interest (Perry & Wise, 1990). Since then, however, conceptualizations have converged more narrowly around an 'emphasis on other orientation – represented by notions of self-sacrifice, altruism and prosocial' (Perry et al., 2010, p. 682). Perry & Hondeghem, (2008, p. 3), for example, include both altruism and pro-social motivation in their PSM definition, stating that PSM is a 'particular form of altruism or prosocial motivation that is animated by specific dispositions and values arising from public institutions and missions'. Conceptually, PSM, pro-social motivation and altruism thus overlap. For our purposes, we understand altruism as an antecedent of PSM (following Esteve et al., 2016) and PSM as a form of pro-social motivation, animated by dispositions and values arising from public organizations and missions. As pro-social motivation is the more general other-regarding motivation and more commonly used in other disciplines – such as psychology (Grant, 2008) and economics (Besley & Ghatak, 2018) – we, however, opt for pro-social motivation rather than PSM in our typology.

Pro-social motivation or PSM (in its pro-social sense) can stem from multiple dimensions. Public employees may be pro-socially motivated due to affection and compassion – that is, due to 'love and concern for others and a desire that others be protected' (Kim & Vandenabeele, 2010, p. 704). Moreover, pro-social motivation may be norm-based. Public servants may identify with and internalize public values – such as fairness, social equity, social justice or social responsibility (see, e.g., Frederickson, 1997, and the discussion of integrated regulation in Section 2.2.1). As a result of this commitment to public values, employees come to value pro-social outcomes. In that sense, work towards pro-social outcomes becomes a calling for public servants, giving them purpose in life (Dobrow & Tosti-Kharas, 2011). Lastly, pro-socially motivated employees may be motivated by self-sacrifice: as Le Grand (2003) argues, degrees of personal sacrifice for others may in and of themselves motivate altruistic behaviour.

Pro-social motivation is often thought to be of particular relevance in the public sector – a stylized fact which has motivated much of the PSM research agenda. Le Grand (2003, p. 35), for instance, concluded that 'it is hard to dispute the view that altruistic motivations are prevalent among providers of public services'.

2.3.4 Commitment to Groups and Organizations

As a last source of motivation in our typology, public employees may be motivated to work hard to attain favorable outcomes for organizations or groups they identify with and are committed to.[9] In line with this logic, a range of studies link organizational commitment to greater job motivation and performance (for a recent review, see Brooks & Wallace, 2006). Next to SDT, this source of motivation can be explicated by, in particular, theories of social identity and organizational commitment.

Social identity theory holds that 'people tend to classify themselves and others into [and thus identify with] various social categories, such as organizational membership, religious affiliation, gender and age cohort' (Ashforth & Mael, 1989, p. 20). These social categories – or identities – come with norms prescribing appropriate behaviour (see, among many, Akerlof & Kranton, 2000). By assuming such group identities, members internalize these norms and regard the group's goals as their own goals. Hard work to attain positive outcomes for an organization or group an employee identifies with thus becomes identity fulfilment (cf. March, 1999). By contrast, poor work effort leads to anxiety associated with losing one's identity (Akerlof & Kranton, 2000) or feelings of shame and group disapproval, for instance (Barr & Serra, 2010).

Organizational and group identification may affect work motivation in both direction and intensity of effort in a manner that is distinct from pro-social motivation. The diverging effect on direction of effort stems from the potential for goal conflicts between identities. Employees typically hold multiple work-related identities: as members of the organization they work for as well as of a profession; an occupation; a union; their department; a political party; or their work group, for instance (Pinder, 2008). While each of these identities may be a source of motivation, they may also conflict. Identification with their peers in a team may, for instance, motivate employees to work hard to foster positive team outcomes. This work effort, however, is directed towards team

---

[9] We employ the term 'organizational commitment' in line with the large academic literature which has developed around this construct (see Meyer, Stanley, Herscovitch & Topolnytsky, 2002). Scholars and practitioners, at times, use related terms such as 'employee attachment' – albeit without a clear conceptual differentiation from 'commitment' (see Pinder, 2008, p. 302).

goals – which may or may not conflict with the goals of the organization or society at large. Corrupt police stations with strong group norms may, for instance, propel police officers to work hard towards the corruption goals of their police station (cf. Hood, James, Peters & Scott, 2004).

Group and organizational identification can also shape work effort above and beyond pro-social motivation. Resh, Marvel & Wen (2018), for instance, show that identification with the mission of a particular organization is a stronger predictor of work effort than pro-social motivation (as measured by self-sacrifice). Baay et al. (2014) in turn show that identification with groups can de-motivate employees where group norms prioritize poor work ethics. Group/organizational identification is thus a distinct source of motivation in our typology. Pro-social motivation motivates work to attain positive outcomes for the public or society as a whole. By contrast, group or organizational identification motivates (or de-motivates) work to attain the goals valued by a smaller group or organization within society.

For the purpose of our typology, attaining these outcomes for a narrower group can also be motivated by self-regarding concerns. Theories of organizational commitment make this explicit. They understand organizational commitment as leading to both a willingness to exert effort to attain the organization's goals and values and a desire to remain a member of the organization (Porter, Steers, Mowday & Boulian, 1974). This commitment is argued to have affective, normative and calculative psychological bases (Meyer & Allen, 1997). Affective commitment refers to emotional ties – and thus, for instance, a sense of pride in membership – an employee develops with an organization or work group. As Akerlof (1984, p. 152) puts it, people 'who work for an institution ... tend to develop sentiment for their co-workers and for that institution'. Normative commitment refers to an internalized sense of obligation towards the organization and its goals, for instance rooted in norms of reciprocity. Both of these other-regarding psychological bases thus relate to the aforementioned social identity and SDT mechanisms. By contrast, a calculative commitment is based on a self-regarding calculation: that the benefits from remaining within an organization are too high to risk expulsion or organizational demise by not working hard towards the organization's (or group's) goals or norms. In that latter sense, calculative organizational commitment approximates 'incentives' in our typology. As organizational (and group) commitment can thus have both other- and self-regarding psychological bases, we locate it on the y-axis between other- and self-regarding motivators in our typology.

Prima facie, public sector organizations offer propitious environments for organizational commitment and identification. Lifelong employment offers greater opportunities for managers to develop an 'esprit de corps' in staff: a feeling of pride and loyalty among staff towards their peer group and a commitment to the organization more generally (Dilulio, 1994; Wilson, 1989). In line with this logic, classic public administration studies suggest that commitment to an organization or group can play important motivating roles in the public sector. Kaufman's (2006) classic study of US forest rangers and Dilulio's (1994) work on the US Federal Bureau of Prisons, for instance, both provide striking examples of 'strong-culture organizations', in which employees are motivated by moral rewards through a 'process of inculcating points of view, fundamental attitudes, loyalties to the organization . . . that will result in subordinating individual interest . . . to the good of the cooperative whole' (Barnard, 1968, pp. 72–4; cited in Dilulio, 1994, p. 283). As a result, employees develop a strong sense of mission: that is, a 'strong belief in the rightness of their task . . . [and] an attachment to the distinctive way of doing things' (Wilson, 1978, pp. 13–14). This sense of mission might, of course, relate to serving the public as a whole, but it also often retains a uniquely organizational element, with convictions about the righteousness of the particular – even if special-interest – goals of an organization. Classic works also suggest that this identification and commitment may materialize at both the organizational and group level. Hood et al. (2004), for instance, show the prevalence of 'mutuality' – peers holding each other to account for their work-related behaviour – in public sector organizations, from the top of the hierarchy among elite groups of civil servants down to street-level bureaucracy where police monitor each other in police patrols. 'Group and organizational commitment' is thus both a distinct motivator and a source of work motivation which might be particularly potent in the public sector.

2.4 Integrating Insights from Other Theories of Work Motivation

Our holistic two-dimensional typologies allowed us to integrate a range of theoretical perspectives and sources of work motivation in the public sector. Our typology, of course, is not the first attempt at bringing together distinct theoretical perspectives and motivators in public administration research. Neumann and Ritz (2015), for instance, differentiate in a three-dimensional model what they term extrinsic, enjoyment-based intrinsic and pro-social intrinsic motivators to explain job (search) preferences; similarly, Andersen, Pedersen & Petersen (2018) conceptualize employee motivation as extrinsic, autonomous or pro-social (see Breaugh, Ritz & Alfes, 2018, among others, for further theoretical integration attempts). Our typology offers the advantage of being both parsimonious – as a two-dimensional framework – and able to draw in a broader set of motivators. Organizational commitment and (more narrow) group identification as a source of motivation, for instance, sit uncomfortably with prior frameworks such as Neumann & Ritz (2015) or Andersen, Pedersen & Petersen (2018), as it neither reflects clearly '(knavish) wage earners' nor 'task nerds' nor 'pro-social white knights' (Andersen et al., 2018, p. 3).

This is, of course, not to say that there are no further theoretical perspectives on work motivation. A comprehensive review exceeds the scope of this Element.[10] In this section, we instead make recourse to several prominent alternative theoretical perspectives to showcase how they can be integrated into – and how their insights further enrich – our typology.

Most strikingly, our typology development has been largely mute on several 'content' theories, which argue that motivation stems from need deficiencies – that is, employees working to satisfy certain innate needs (Rainey, 2014, p. 269). Prominently, Maslow (1954) had argued for a hierarchy of five innate needs, from physiological needs (e.g. relief from hunger) at the very bottom to safety needs (freedom from bodily harm) to social needs (e.g. affection, belonging to social groups) to self-esteem needs (e.g. achievement, prestige) to self-actualization needs on top (fulfilling one's potential). In his theory, unsatisfied needs dominate behaviour – that is, higher-order needs can only motivate once lower-order needs are met. Maslow's (1954) theory is helpful in pointing to the variety of needs of humans, including a need for self-actualization. Particularly in developing countries, where public sector pay is often insufficient to meet basic household needs (Meyer-Sahling, Schuster & Mikkelsen, 2018), the theory also points to the importance of satisfying basic physiological and safety needs to safeguard public employee motivation (but see Tendler & Freedheim, 1994). Researchers seeking to empirically verify the five-step hierarchy have, however, not found empirical support for it (cf. Pinder, 2008). As a result, our own typology does, contrary to Maslow (1954), not impose any hierarchy of motivators. It usefully builds on Maslow (1954), however, in considering that different individuals have different needs and motivators and that management practice needs to adapt to them.

Building on Maslow, Herzberg (1968) prominently proposed a two-factor theory, which argued that work motivation is a function of 'motivators' and 'hygiene factors'. Addressing hygiene factors – such as poor working conditions, bad relations to colleagues or poor pay – ensures that 'basic

---

[10] Interested readers can turn to Pinder (2008), Mitchell (1982) and Kanfer (1990) for more detailed overviews.

survival' or maintenance needs are addressed, including a need to avoid pain, hunger and discomfort. Addressing these needs can prevent job dissatisfaction; it cannot, however, motivate staff to work hard in Herzberg's (1968) theory. By contrast, 'motivators' – such as achievement, recognition or advancement – are argued to motivate hard work by addressing growth needs: they enable employees to become all that they can be. For our purposes, Herzberg (1968) is a helpful reminder that the six motivators in our typology are not only potential sources of motivation but also potential sources of de-motivation. To illustrate, an interesting job can make work intrinsically enjoyable and thus motivate staff to work hard, just as a dull job can make work intrinsically non-enjoyable and thus de-motivate staff. In our typology, each of our motivators can thus equally act as a potential de-motivator. Contrary to Herzberg (1968), however, we do not classify them into 'motivator' and 'hygiene' factors. The rationale is simple: this differentiation is not robustly supported empirically (cf. Pinder, 2008, p. 37).

Our typology can also be helpfully combined with insights from equity theory (Adams, 1965). Equity theory is based on a need for fairness; employees seek to maintain a fair balance between their contribution to an organization (inputs, such as their education, skills and work effort) and what they get in return (outputs, such as wages or skill development). Employees determine whether inputs and outputs are fairly balanced by comparing themselves to colleagues and friends and their respective input–output ratios. If they perceive inequity relative to others, they seek to resolve this tension by adjusting their inputs – for instance, by lowering their work effort if they sense they are underpaid. This sense of fairness and equity thereby matters in regards to not only outputs employees are receiving but also the decision-making procedures that determined these outcomes, for instance 'the dignity and respect demonstrated in the course of presenting an undesirable outcome' (Greenberg & Baron, 2003, p. 205).[11] For the purposes of our typology, equity theory is a helpful reminder that motivators of public employees are ultimately perception-contingent. For instance, whether an output such as pay motivates or de-motivates public employees ultimately hinges not only on their objective pay levels but also on the perceptions that employees form of their pay (Meyer-Sahling, Schuster & Mikkelsen, 2018). This puts a premium on taking the perception basis of the motivators in our typology seriously. Motivation thus depends not only on the choice of intervention to enhance outputs (that is,

---

[11] In that sense, equity theory also relates to psychological contract theory, which argues that employees engage in social – not only contractual – exchanges with their employer, with mutual respect for each other's motives (see Mitchell, 1982).

'motivators' in our typology) – for instance a job re-design – but also on how managers communicate motivation-enhancing interventions, including whether such communications are credible in light of past manager–employee interactions (cf. Andersen et al., 2018). Equity theory also implies that, while motivational practices necessarily require adaptation to what motivates a given individual employee, the employee's response to these motivational efforts will depend in part on her perception of what her manager or organization is doing to motivate her colleagues. Motivational practices thus need to be adapted to individual needs, values and attitudes while retaining a semblance of fairness and equity across colleagues.

In short, our typology and its application can be usefully enhanced by incorporating insights from needs-based theories of work motivation. They underscore that different individuals have different needs and motivators and that management practice needs to adapt to them; that motivators in our typology should be understood as both potential sources of motivation and potential sources of *de*-motivation; and that the effect of motivational practices ultimately depends on how employees perceive them. Credible communication by managers and a fair application of motivational (and other) practices between colleagues shape their effects.

2.5 Integrating the Typology into Management Practice

While our typology is mute on specific management practices to enhance our six motivators – Section 4 will discuss these practices in-depth – it nonetheless entails several implications for practice.

First and most obviously, our typology implies that motivation does not stop with self-interested carrots and sticks (incentives) – the focus of classic economic theories of bureaucracy. It also does not stop with pro-social motivation or PSM – which, as we show in Section 3, has been the most studied motivator in public administration research. Rather, it requires managers to consider the range of potential other- and self-regarding and extrinsic and intrinsic motivators – including, beyond incentives and pro-social motivation, the creation of enjoyable jobs and working conditions, the promotion of relatedness between colleagues, the strengthening of team and organizational commitment, and the creation of opportunities for public servants to sense a 'warm glow' (Figure 3).

As prior research is inconclusive (cf. Pinder, 2008), our typology does not assume that any of these six motivators is more or less effective – with one important qualification. Motivation is determined by not only intensity but also direction of work effort. As noted, other-regarding motivators – and in

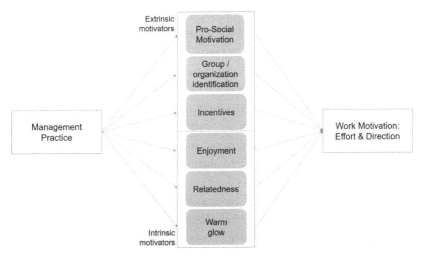

Figure 3 Management practice and work motivation in the public sector

particular pro-social motivation – might more easily translate into work effort directed towards organizational and public interests than self-regarding motivators. With that caveat in mind, managers need to consider how to maximize those motivators which most matter for *their* employees, given their unique needs, values and attitudes. Effective motivation of public employees thus requires an understanding not only of motivational techniques but also of individual staff members and what ultimately matters to and motivates them – for instance, whether they are other- and/or self-regarding and outcome- and/or activity-motivated.

Adaptation to individual needs, attitudes and values, of course, does not mean that managers should take these as fixed. Rather – and as several of the management practices in Sections 3 and 4 further substantiate – needs, attitudes and values can be shaped by organizations. In other words, effective motivation is as much about adapting management practices to what most motivates a given employee as it is about shifting these employee preferences towards the motivators – such as pro-social motivation and organizational commitment – which managers can most (cost-)effectively enhance.

Figure 3 also implies that managers need to assess the motivational implications of a given management practice on all motivators in our typology concurrently. A given management practice may foster one form of motivation while curbing another. Strengthening a given motivator may thus do more harm than good if it concurrently and disproportionately curbs another motivator. In other words, management practices often cause trade-offs between motivators. The most prominent example for such trade-offs is what Frey and Osterloh

(2002) term 'crowding out'. The introduction of an extrinsic incentive – such as performance-related pay – may, for instance, reduce task enjoyment if it is perceived as controlling and thus lowers the sense of autonomy and independence of employees. Extrinsic incentives may also crowd out pro-social motivation by reducing the sense of self-sacrifice of employees for society and by shifting their work objective from helping society to attaining performance pay (Le Grand, 2003). On top, extrinsic, individualized performance incentives may crowd out employees' identification with team goals by incentivizing them to prioritize individually attributable performance (Hood et al., 2004).

Vice versa, however, management practices may also have positive multiplier effects, enhancing one form of motivation, which in turn fosters others. In other words, motivators may 'crowd in' other motivators. Extrinsic incentives and control systems, for instance, may crowd in other motivators where the intervention is seen as supportive and 'self-esteem is fostered, and individuals feel that they are given more freedom to act, thus enlarging self-determination' (Frey & Jegen, 2001, p. 595). Receiving performance rewards may, for instance, bolster individual self-esteem and organizational commitment where they signal the organization's benevolence towards the employee (Osterloh & Frey, 2013). This implies not only that the dividing line between different motivators is not always clear-cut but also – more importantly – that management practices targeting one motivator may concurrently crowd in and crowd out other motivators. Managers thus need to assess potential crowding in and out of motivators before introducing a new motivational practice – that is, they need to consider trade-offs in their motivational approach.

At the same time – and as aforementioned – managers need to consider how their motivational practice shapes not only the employee(s) it seeks to motivate but also others in the organization. Motivating *some* employees can change whether *others* perceive equity and fairness in how the organization is treating them. In short, managers need to consider both intended and unintended consequences of motivational practices for different motivators of both their employees and others in the organization.

In doing so, they also need to remain aware that management practices are only one – among many – determinants of workforce motivation. Parental, educational and religious socialization since childhood can, for instance, shape the extent to which individuals are pro-socially motivated – and thus the extent to which a pro-socially motivated pool of potential public sector applicants exists (Perry, 1997). More generally, we can think of the motivators in our typology as resulting from individual, job-level, team-level, organizational-level and societal-level factors (see Figure 4; see also Perry & Porter, 1982).

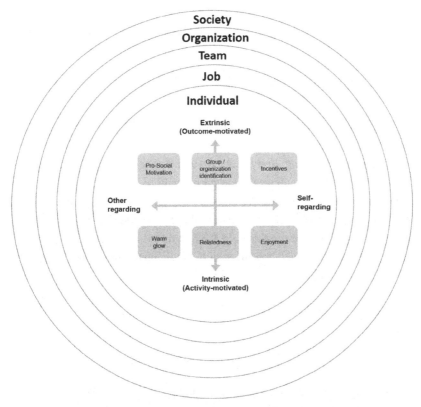

Figure 4 The determinants of work motivation in the public sector at differential levels

Only some of these factors are under managerial control. Mid-level managers may, for instance, re-design jobs to enhance their motivating potential or strengthen group cohesion through team work; high-level managers might introduce organization-wide pay-for-performance schemes to enhance extrinsic incentives or company nurseries to strengthen organizational commitment. Managers can also, to some extent, shape individual-level determinants by changing who the organization recruits or retains. Other factors which potentially shape public sector work motivation, however – such as the societal prestige of bureaucracy, the pool of potential applicants in the labour market and the clarity of legislative mandates for public sector organizations – are to a significant degree outside managerial control. Motivating public employees thus implies maximizing the motivational potential of the subset of motivation determinants which public managers can, in fact, shape.

In the next section, we will systematically review the public administration literature to disentangle which precise determinants and management practices are associated with greater work motivation in the public sector.

3 Lessons from Public Administration Research about Work Motivators in the Public Sector

In this section, we review public administration research on the determinants of work motivation in the public sector. As noted, while reviews of the determinants of PSM abound (e.g. Perry et al., 2010), no prior study has systematically and comprehensively reviewed the determinants of work motivation in the public sector more generally. As a result, we do not have a clear empirical picture of why some public servants are more motivated to work hard than others. This section takes on this task. We first discuss the methodology of our review. Subsequently, we show what public administration research has substantively, regionally and methodologically studied in public sector work motivation – and what not. We then move to the core of the section, reviewing evidence on the determinants of work motivation in the public sector from public administration research.

3.1 Literature Review Methodology

We reviewed the public administration literature in three steps. We, first, looked for studies which seek to explain work motivation in the public sector in general (with the keyword 'motivation' in the abstract). Noting that a series of studies operationalize work motivation with individual performance measures, we proceeded with a search for studies which seek to explain individual performance of public employees (with the keywords 'performance', 'job performance' and 'work performance'). Third, and in line with our typology, we complemented this search on the determinants of work motivation with a search on the determinants of individual motivators in our typology, using the following keywords: 'organizational commitment', 'group commitment', 'organizational identification', 'group identification', 'incentive(s)', 'intrinsic motivation', 'warm glow', 'enjoyment', and 'relatedness'. As PSM has recently seen a comprehensive review (Ritz et al., 2016), we did not conduct a separate PSM literature search but rather included Ritz et al.'s (2016) review of antecedents of PSM in our analysis.[12]

---

[12] The entries for the column on the antecedents of PSM for Tables 3 to 6 are thus taken from Ritz et al. (2016). Note that their review is broader: it includes employees outside the public sector and a broader set of journals, including journals outside public administration. Our findings should be read with this caveat in mind.

Using the database Proquest, we searched for studies published up to September 2018 for these keywords in the title or abstract of articles published in twelve leading public administration journals: *Journal of Public Administration Research and Theory, Public Administration Review, Public Administration, Governance, International Public Management Journal, Public Management Review, American Review of Public Administration, Public Performance and Management Review, International Review of Administrative Sciences, Review of Public Personnel Administration, Administration and Society,* and *Public Personnel Management.* While our search does not cover all public administration journals, our coverage of leading public administration journals and public personnel administration journals allows us to plausibly identify the bulk of rigorous public administration research on work motivation in the public sector.

Of the studies identified with these keywords, we included in our review only those assessing determinants of work motivation (rather than, for instance, its consequences). Moreover, we focused our review in line with this Element's interest on samples of public servants – excluding results for employees from other sectors (non-profit or private sector). Multi-sector studies which did not offer differentiated results for public employees were thus similarly excluded.[13]

3.2 Public Sector Work Motivation: What Has Public Administration Research Studied?

In total, we identified 141 studies in our systematic literature review, in addition to 88 studies on the determinants of PSM in Ritz et al. (2016). Out of the 141 studies, our review identified 95 public administration studies which have assessed the determinants of work motivation (55) and individual performance (40). Given the overlap in measurements of the two in public administration research, we include both in our review. As the two concepts differ, however – individual performance depends not only on work motivation, but also other factors such as ability and resources – we will review the determinants of each rather than treating them as a single dependent variable.

---

[13] We organized this review in a database containing for each study: author(s), year of publication, title, link to the article, journal name, method used, sample (region/country/institution), number of observations, theoretical framework used (if any), definition of work motivation, measure of work motivation, and determinants of (or practices to enhance) work motivation, with positive effects, insignificant effects and negative effects. The list of studies included in our review is available in the Technical Appendix of this Element: see www.cambridge.org/mpe.

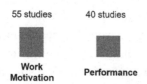

Figure 5 Determinants of work motivation: number of studies by keyword

Multiple classifications are possible where studies assess the determinants of multiple motivators in a single study or an individual motivator and work motivation as a whole.

Out of all studies in our *and* in Ritz et al.'s (2016) review, a total of 161 assessed the determinants of individual motivators in our typology (rather than of work motivation or performance). More than half of these (88) study why some public employees have more PSM than others. PSM has thus been the dominant motivator of study in public administration research. In fact, there have been almost as many studies of the determinants of PSM as of work motivation *and* individual performance in the public sector. Beyond PSM, public administration research has paid significant attention to a second motivator in our typology: sixty studies assess the determinants of organizational commitment, organizational identification, group identification or group commitment.

The determinants of the remaining motivators, by contrast, remain understudied. Only seven studies have looked at why some public employees find their jobs more intrinsically enjoyable than others. Three have looked at why some public servants sense greater relatedness at work with colleagues, and three more at why some public servants perceive greater incentives at work than others. None has explicitly assessed why some public servants sense greater 'warm glow' than others.

Of course, studies assess these motivators not only in terms of their determinants (Figure 6) but also in terms of their effect on work motivation. Figure 6 thus does not contain all studies involving these motivators. A subset of the 95 studies assessing the determinants of work motivation or performance (Figure 5) looks to these motivators as explanators – estimating, for instance, the effect of different pay incentive schemes on motivation. Section 3.3 will discuss these studies in depth. With that qualification in mind, our overview does suggest that, in terms of our two-dimensional typology, public administration research has been highly unbalanced. Studies of individual motivators have paid much greater attention to determinants of extrinsic motivators (151 studies) than intrinsic motivators (10 studies) and to determinants of purely other-regarding motivators (88 studies) rather than purely self-regarding motivators (10 studies).

Table 1 Country focus of studies on the determinants of public sector work motivation

Country	Freq.	%	Country	Freq.	%
United States	82	56.94	Thailand	2	1.39
South Korea	9	6.25	Israel	2	1.39
The Netherlands	8	5.56	France	1	0.69
United Kingdom	7	4.86	Brazil	1	0.69
China	6	4.17	Egypt	1	0.69
Italy	6	4.17	Ghana	1	0.69
Taiwan	5	3.47	Spain	1	0.69
Belgium	5	3.47	Switzerland	1	0.69
Denmark	3	2.08	Vietnam	1	0.69
Australia	2	1.39	**Total**	**144**	**100**

This table does not include studies of PSM as Ritz et al. (2016)'s review does not disaggregate geographic origin data for studies of the determinants of PSM.

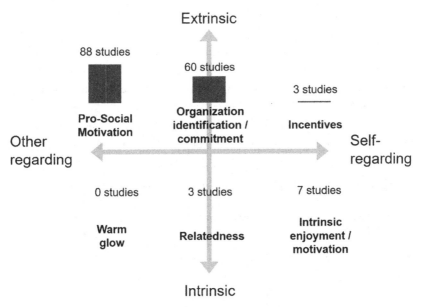

Figure 6 Determinants of work motivators: number of studies

Lack of balance in research focus extends not only to the motivators studied, but also the regional focus of research (see Table 1). Most studies draw on US samples (57 per cent), followed by Europe (20 per cent of studies) and three countries in East Asia (South Korea, China and Taiwan) (14 per cent). The remaining 9 per cent of studies cover the rest of the globe. Public sector work motivation in much of the developing world – Africa, Latin America, the Middle East, South and Central Asia – thus remains largely unstudied. As a result, we know little about the effects of different administrative traditions and country characteristics on public sector work motivators. Do government employees in Peru respond equally to pay-for-performance schemes as civil servants in Whitehall? If not, which are the factors explaining these differences? Future studies should consider how different cultural, organizational and administrative traditions interact with the determinants of work motivation.

3.3 How Has Public Administration Research Studied Work Motivation?

To date, studies of work motivation draw overwhelmingly on quantitative observational research (81 per cent) – using, in particular, bivariate, multiple, logistic and SEM models (Table 2). By contrast, qualitative works on public sector work motivation remain scarce (12 per cent of studies) – though this share remains above the average proportion of qualitative studies in top public administration journals (see Ospina, Esteve & Seulki, 2018). Similar, studies based on experimental inferences (4 per cent) remain – as in public administration at large – the exception, with only seven studies relying on experimental and quasi-experimental designs to infer causality between motivation and its determinants.

In sum, the heavy reliance on observational data raises serious concerns about the validity of findings from public administration research about

Table 2 Methods used to study the determinants of public sector work motivation

Method[a]	Freq.	%[b]
Bivariate Measures of association or tests of differences	11	6.71
Multivariate, SEM cross-sectional, SEM panel Multiple regression (including multilevel, panel)	122	74.39
Experimental Designs	7	4.27
A qualitative analytical technique	20	12.20
Other	4	2.44
Total	158	100.00

* Multiple classifications per study were possible. Percentages are the share of the total number of times methods were used. Table excludes PSM studies as Ritz et al. (2016)'s review does not disaggregate methods used for studies of the determinants of PSM.

public sector work motivation. Many of the core explanators we review in the next section are susceptible to omitted variable bias. Organizations, for instance, might plausibly react to low work motivation by introducing pay-for-performance or re-designing jobs. Studies correlating pay-for-performance or job re-designs with lower work motivation thus arguably hardly enable valid inferences about the effects of pay-for-performance or job design. This holds all the more as almost all studies draw on survey questionnaires for both independent and dependent variables. Common method bias – or variance – is thus likely to occur, further biasing results (see, for a discussion, Jacobsen & Jensen, 2015). Our discussion of the determinants of public sector work motivation in the next section should be read with this caveat in mind.

A second important caveat to this discussion is heterogeneity in the conceptualization and measurement of work motivation. If those differ, then studies ultimately explain different conceptualizations of work motivation. Inconsistent findings might thus simply result from looking at the determinants of two different conceptualizations.

This risk is inherent in studies of work motivation for two reasons in particular. First, work motivation is a multidimensional concept (see Section 2.1), albeit with contestation around the precise conceptualizations of these dimensions. Some studies conceptualize work motivation as the intensity, persistence and direction of behaviour – albeit with varying terminology (e.g. Mitchell, 1982; Perry & Porter, 1982; Kanfer, 1990). Others – including this Element – collapse the conceptualization of work motivation into two dimensions: the intensity and direction of work effort. This lack of consensus on conceptualization is paralleled by an even greater lack of consensus on measurement. Contrary to PSM (see Perry, 1996; Kim et al., 2012) and organizational commitment (see Meyer & Allen, 1997), there is no widely accepted measurement scale for work motivation in general and public sector work motivation in particular. Studies thus use varying measures, from subjective single measures such as 'I feel a higher degree of motivation toward my position as compared with one year ago' (Paarlberg, 2007, p. 210); to multidimensional measures such as the four-item 'I put forth my best effort to get the job done regardless of the difficulties'; 'Time seems to drag while I am on the job'; 'It has been hard for me to get very involved in my current job'; and 'I do extra work for my job that isn't really expected of me' (Chen & Bozeman, 2013) This variation might in part be explained by the scant research assessing the validity – including predictive validity – of distinct work motivation measures in the public sector. Whether any of the used measures are valid thus remains an open question. What is clear, however, is that all typically seek to measure the intensity of work effort – rather than a more multidimensional conceptualization of work motivation which also includes direction. The lack of a widely accepted measure of work motivation might explain in part why public administration scholars have – in comparison to PSM and organizational commitment – paid relatively less attention to it. Variation in measurement, of course, also requires the aforementioned caution when interpreting the results in the next section: inconsistent findings might stem from inconsistent measurement.

3.4 The Determinants of Work Motivation in the Public Sector

As noted in Section 2, work motivation can stem from individual, job-level, management/team-level, organizational-level and societal-level factors. We follow these levels to structure our review, discussing, first, evidence for individual-level determinants of public sector work motivation (demographic factors and attitudes, values and traits of individual employees). Subsequently, we review evidence on job-level determinants, management/team-level determinants and organizational-level determinants respectively. Research on societal-level determinants is close to non-existent, precluding a separate section on it.

We review the evidence on each of these sets of determinants for both work motivation as a whole (measured by work motivation or individual performance) and for each of the motivators in our typology (PSM, organizational commitment and intrinsic motivation). The lack of significant public administration research on warm glow and relatedness precludes us from drawing inferences about their determinants.

3.4.1 Demographic Determinants of Work Motivation

Though a range of demographic factors have been discussed in prior studies (Table 3), the bulk of studies has focused on three demographic antecedents: age, gender and education. The evidence on these antecedents is mixed. Looking at all of our dependent variables together, the majority of studies on age, gender and education has found insignificant effects – rather than positive or negative effects. More often than not, demographic antecedents thus do not appear to be significant drivers of public sector work motivation. In a subset of studies, however, they do matter; and theoretical arguments linking demographics to motivation certainly do exist. In a given organization, demographics can thus play a role in work motivation. On balance, the evidence thereby suggests that women and older public servants are – where demographic factors are significant – more likely to have superior work motivation, PSM and organizational commitment.

Age has thereby been the most studied variable. Are older public servants more motivated? The evidence on PSM and organizational commitment is

Table 3 Demographic determinants of work motivation

Antecedents	Work motivation						Individual motivators									TOTAL	
	Measure: work motivation			Measure: individual performance			Intrinsic motivation			Public service motivation			Org. commit. & identification				
	Sig. +ive	Sig. -ive	Not sig	Sig. +ive	Sig. -ive	Not sig	Sig. +ive	Sig. -ive	Not sig	Sig. +ive	Sig. -ive	Not sig	Sig. +ive	Sig. -ive	Not sig	Freq.	%
Demographics																	
Age	8	2	13	1	2	5				28	6	22	11	2	16	116	8.81
Gender (female)	12	2	5	5	1	10	0	0	2	16	9	39	6	3	0	110	8.36
Education	0	3	8				0	0	2	17	6	22	2	0	12	72	5.47
Race (white)	7	1	6	4	2	7				2	2	11	1	1	2	46	3.50
Married	2	1	3	1	0	0				2	0	3	0	1	2	15	1.14
Religiousness										5	0	4				9	0.68
Membership in association or union										3	0	3				6	0.46
Membership in volunteer organization/volunteering										4	0	1				5	0.38
Kids	0	0	2	1	1	0							1	0	1	4	0.30
Other	2	0	1	1	1	0							0	0	2	7	0.53

* Multiple classifications per study were possible. Percentages are the share of the total determinants tested. Number of times that statistically significant positive, negative and insignificant associations were found.

Source: Our own literature review and, with adaptations, Ritz et al. (2016).

strongest; of the studies which find significant effects, thirty-nine find positive effects and eight find negative effects. This might, for instance, be explained by attrition: younger public servants less motivated to serve the public and committed to their organization leave the public sector, while only the more motivated and committed ones remain and grow old in the organization. It might also be due to generational differences, with younger generations potentially being more cynical of the idea of serving the society (Moynihan & Pandey, 2007), or by psychological processes associated with growing old, with a more pronounced tendency to embrace traditional values and a supportive work ethic (Ting, 1997).

At the same time, the evidence for an effect of age on work motivation and performance is less consistent – with nine studies identifying positive effects and four identifying negative effects. Theoretically, there are good reasons to expect mixed effects. Greater PSM and organizational commitment may enhance work motivation. At the same time, incentives change. To name a few, old age comes with fewer prospects for career progression and – with children having left home – less of a need for income progression to maintain one's household (Warr, 2001). Moreover, biological factors change. As we grow older, our fluid and crystalized ability tends to diminish, which affects exerted effort and may lead to compensation strategies (Kanfer & Ackerman, 2004). Empirically, mixed effects might also stem from confounding factors which correlate with age and shape motivators but are hard to control for (such as differential retirement plans) and from non-linear effects: work motivation might change in certain periods of life – e.g. during early childhood periods of children – rather than linearly with age. Yet, the studies reviewed all estimated linear effects.

Gender is the second most studied demographic antecedent. Contrary to age, the relationship of gender to work motivation (and performance) is somewhat more consistent than the relationship with PSM and organizational commitment. Seventeen studies find positive effects of women on work motivation/performance; only three find negative effects. At the same time, twenty-two find positive effects for PSM and organizational commitment; twelve find negative effects. Why would female public employees be more motivated to work hard? One possible explanation is expectancy. Female employees are argued to have lower expectations about their working conditions than males; poor working conditions are thus less likely to de-motivate them (Clark, 1997). A second possible explanation – among others – is compassion; DeHart-Davis et al. (2006) argue that women are more compassionate and thus eager to work hard in favour of their societies. Counterarguments do exist, however.

Public sector organizations have been critiqued for being more culturally masculine than other organizations (Duerst-Lahti & Johnston, 1990). As a result, negative biases against female employees might de-motivate them – particularly in countries outside the West with traditionally higher levels of labour-market segregation. The effect of gender on work motivation is thus likely to be context-dependent. Moreover, the theorized mechanisms are often not strongly evidenced; whether the relation between gender and motivation is shaped biologically or culturally (or both) thus remains to some extent unknown.

Education is the third most studied demographic antecedent. Empirically, somewhat surprisingly, not a single study associates higher education levels with greater work motivation/performance (with three studies finding negative effects and eight studies finding no effect). The link to PSM and organizational commitment is more positive, with nineteen studies finding a positive effect and six a negative effect. A range of theorized mechanisms might account for these differential effects. Kim and Rubianty (2011), for instance, explains the negative (or null) effect of education by pointing to labour market opportunities: more educated respondents are more able to find outside jobs and have greater job mobility and, thus, might be less committed to and working hard for any given employer. The differential effect on PSM has, similarly, seen a range of theorized explanations. Perry et al. (2008), for instance, argued that education leads to greater pro-social volunteering in life, which in turn increases awareness of the importance of working to help societies.

Overall then, the data does not support strong generalizations about the role of demographic factors in public sector work motivation. There are competing theoretical arguments linking these factors to higher and lower motivation; and, empirically, most studies do not find any effect. Female and older employees are more often than not more committed and motivated to work hard and serve society – but the opposite can, on occasion, be equally the case. While demographic factors thus remain important controls, other antecedents offer more leverage to practitioners and avenues for future research.

3.4.2 Attitudes, Values and Traits Influencing Public Sector Work Motivation

As a very distinct type of individual-level antecedents, we now turn to attitudes, values and personality traits of public employees.

These, first of all, provide evidence for the relevance of the motivators in our typology and underscore the potential for virtuous cycles (one motivator spurring others). For instance, five studies identify a positive effect of organizational commitment on work motivation (two studies) and PSM (three studies).[14] Fifteen out of twenty-one studies in turn find positive effects of extrinsic (focused on incentives) and intrinsic (focused on enjoyment) work motivation on performance, PSM and organizational commitment (only one study finds a negative effect).

Beyond underscoring the plausibility of our typology, studies of attitudes, values and traits point to several significant determinants of public sector work motivation: job and organizational satisfaction; trust in managers; and a perception of self-efficacy.

Satisfaction of employees with their jobs or organization are, perhaps unsurprisingly, associated with greater organizational commitment (thirteen studies), work motivation (five studies) and performance (two studies). Only two studies find no effect, and a single study finds a negative effect. These positive linkages are theoretically intuitive: job satisfaction is the result of an affective relation with the organization, in which employees feel that there is a strong connection with an organization and organizational members, which then leads to positive reactions to the job, such as being more motivated.

Similarly, trust in managers has positive effects. Fourteen studies associate it with greater organizational commitment; three associate it with greater work motivation; and three studies find no effect. This relationship is theoretically intuitive. To illustrate one potential theoretical mechanism: 'as supervisors are often personified as the "face" or "representative" of the organization, responsible for implementing organizational policy, positive treatment by supervisors should lead subordinates to reciprocate in the form of desired work attitudes such as organizational commitment' (Miao et al., 2014, p. 731).

A further attitudinal determinant with typically positive effects is self-efficacy – an employee's belief in his or her ability to accomplish a work-related task successfully. Seven of twelve studies identify positive effects of self-efficacy; two identify negative effects (particularly with organizational commitment). Several mechanisms link self-efficacy to greater work motivation. First, high self-efficacy individuals are more likely to believe that performance goals can be achieved and to persist with efforts towards goal attainment (Wright, 2004). Moreover, employees tend to enjoy more those activities in which they perform well – feeling reassured, happier and more engaged with tasks they can do well relative to those they cannot (Bellé & Cantarelli, 2015). Self-efficacy, however, is not always a driver of motivation – hence the potential for negative effects. In some instances, employees with high levels of self-efficacy can be

---

[14] Moreover, two studies find a positive effect of job commitment on performance (with a third study finding no effect).

bored with their jobs, if these are not perceived as challenging (Moynihan & Pandey, 2007). Self-efficacy can thus enhance work motivation where it enables employees to perform tasks they are good at – but only if these tasks do not cause boredom as a result. The implication for job design is clear: design job tasks that are sufficiently challenging to avoid boredom but not so challenging as to undermine a sense of self-efficacy. We return to this implication in our discussion of job-level factors in the next section.

Two further variables have seen a relevant number of studies assessing their effects on PSM. First, three of six studies associate left-wing political ideology with greater PSM (with one finding the opposite). A greater propensity towards social activism and volunteering might mediate this effect (Ritz et al., 2016). Second, professional identification has been linked to greater PSM in two of four studies (with two studies finding no effect). Professional identification is the sense of identification of employees with their profession – such as doctors, teachers, police or firefighters. Theoretically, inconsistent effects of professional identification on PSM may be very much expected; effects depend on whether the profession employees identify with is pro-social and providing them with a public service ethic which reinforces pro-social motivation (Pandey & Stazyk, 2008).

Table 4 shows the panoply of other potential attitudes, values or personality traits which have been studied. We have focused our review on the antecedents with the greatest number of supporting studies. Space constraints preclude us from discussing the remainder. With that caveat in mind, what our review does suggest is that work motivation is significantly affected by other attitudes, values and traits of public servants. Satisfaction with jobs and the organization; trust in management; a sense of self-efficacy; and, to a lesser extent, identification with one's profession and political ideology all shape the motivation of public servants. The implication for management practice is clear: managers need to assess how their interventions affect not only work motivation directly but also other attitudes and values of public servants – such as trust in management – which affect their motivation.

3.4.3 Job-Level Determinants of Work Motivation

Contrary to demographics, attitudes, values and traits, job-level factors can be directly manipulated by organizations – they are thus of particular interest from a management perspective. In line with this reasoning, public administration scholars have paid significant attention to them (see Table 5). Five sets of factors have seen most research: organizational tenure; rank; pay and benefits; job design (in particular, goal setting, feedback, empowerment, teamwork, task

Table 4 Attitudes, values and traits influencing work motivation

Antecedents	Work motivation			Individual performance			Intrinsic motivation			Public service motivation			Org. commit. & identification			TOTAL	
	Sig. +ive	Sig. -ive	Not sig	Sig. +ive	Sig. -ive	Not sig	Sig. +ive	Sig. -ive	Not sig	Sig. +ive	Sig. -ive	Not sig	Sig. +ive	Sig. -ive	Not sig.	Freq.	%
Attitudes, values and traits																	
Intrinsic or extrinsic motivation				2	0	2				0	1	1	13	0	2	21	1.60
Trust (managerial)	3	0	1	5	0	1							14	0	2	20	1.60
PSM				2	0	1							12	0	2	20	1.52
Job satisfaction													13	1	1	18	1.37
Self-efficacy	5	1	1	1	0	0	1	0	0				1	2	0	12	0.91
Political attitude (0 = left, 1 = right)										1	3	2				6	0.46
Org. involvement/commitment	2	0	1							3	0	0				6	0.46
Organizational satisfaction	5	0	0													5	0.38
Professional identification										2	0	2				4	0.30
Emotional intelligence				1	1	1							0	0	1	4	0.23
Job commitment				2	0	1							0	1	1	3	0.15
Interest in Money													1	1	0	2	0.15
Psychological contract fulfilment																2	0.15

Burnout	0	2	0	2	0.08
Political skills	1	0	1	2	0.08
Psychological needs satisfaction	1	0	1	2	0.08
Desire for responsibility	1	0	0	1	0.08
Task-oriented values	1	0	0	1	0.08
Self-actualization	1	0	0	1	0.08
Sense of humour	1	0	0	1	0.08
Dependability	1	0	0	1	0.08
Tendency to speak up	1	0	0	1	0.08
Proper comportment	1	0	0	1	0.08
Emotional suppression	0	0	1	1	0.08
Interpersonal harmony	1	0	0	1	1.60
Locus of control	1	0	0	1	1.60
Positive affect	1	0	0	1	1.52

* Multiple classifications per study were possible. Percentages are the share of the total determinants tested. Number of times that statistically significant positive, negative and insignificant associations were found.

Source: Our own literature review and, with adaptations, Ritz et al. (2016).

motivation and task significance); and traditional human resource management practices (in particular, training and job security).

Tenure is the most studied determinant (eighty-eight studies). Its effect on work motivation/performance as a whole is mixed – though more often than not it has negative (eight studies) rather than positive (five studies) effects. The same holds for its effect on organizational commitment, with nine studies identifying positive and ten identifying negative effects (and seventeen identifying no effects). Why would public employees who choose to remain within their organization (and thus have longer tenure) become less committed to it and less motivated to work hard? Several theoretical rationales have been posited. For example, Carson and Carson (1997) argue that 'career entrenchment' can foster career dissatisfaction. Greater organizational tenure enhances the costs of quitting, leaving individuals stuck in jobs even as they become less satisfied and less engaged. Vigoda (2000), among others, in turn argues that over time public employees discover and become disillusioned with organizational politics, with negative effects on organizational commitment. At the same time, however, our review also shows that tenure is more likely than not to be associated with greater PSM (eight positive, one negative) – though most studies (twenty-six) find no effect. Organizational socialization into public sector values during a public sector career might account for this (Crewson, 1997). Since public sector values relate to helping society, socialization into these values with greater public sector tenure can thus lead to higher PSM. Overall, then, organizational tenure has complex effects on work motivation, both theoretically and empirically. Where it has an effect, it is more likely than not to be associated with lower work motivation and organizational commitment yet higher PSM. In more than half of studies, however, it does *not* have a significant effect. Other job-level determinants might thus be more consistent levers for managers seeking to enhance work motivation.

The second most widely studied job-level determinant is managerial rank. Are managers more motivated than employees? Our review suggests that, more often than not, they are. They exhibit greater motivation/performance in six studies (versus two studies with negative effects); greater PSM in twelve studies (versus three studies with negative effects); and greater organizational commitment in ten studies (versus six studies with negative effects). Theoretically, this is not implausible. Supervisory status typically comes with greater responsibility for achieving organizational goals and a greater perception of trust by high-level managers who promoted the employee to management (cf. Pitts, 2009). Both of these factors might enhance work motivation. Empirically, however, these effects are far from a foregone conclusion. Roughly 30 per cent of studies find no significant effects of managerial rank. More importantly, cross-sectional statistical associations do not provide plausible evidence for a causal effect of managerial rank. Employees might have been promoted to a managerial rank precisely because they are more motivated and performing (Andersen, Kristensen & Pedersen, 2015). The statistical associations might thus merely reflect selection bias in who gets promoted – rather than an effect of rank. In short, management responsibilities are more likely to be associated with greater work motivation than not – though they almost equally often have no effect. Whether these associations are causal remains unclear.

Pay (fifty-seven studies) and benefits (thirty-two studies) have been the third most studied set of job-level factors. These studies have, in broad terms, assessed the effects of pay levels as well as performance pay and benefits such as pensions or childcare. More often than not, higher pay and greater benefits are associated with greater work motivation and performance (thirty-six studies with positive effects, seven with negative effects); greater PSM (four studies with positive effects, one with negative effects); and greater organizational commitment (eight studies with positive effects, one with negative effects). Roughly 30 per cent of studies find no significant effects. (Higher) pay and benefits thus *can* enhance work motivation. Theoretically, there are several plausible explanations for this. To name a few, Herzberg (1968) classically argued that low pay acts as a hygienic factor which dissatisfies and de-motivates staff (though the evidence on his two-factor theory is thin; cf. Pinder, 2008, p. 37). Moreover, higher pay might attract more motivated staff into the public sector (Dal Bó, Finan & Rossi, 2013) or enable organizations to retain more motivated staff, which is often precisely the group of staff with better outside labour market opportunities (Meyer-Sahling, Schuster & Mikkelsen, 2018). In addition, benefits such as pensions, childcare or medical insurance might – in line with social exchange theory – enhance organizational commitment of (grateful) employees to their organization and thus work motivation (Caillier, 2013).

These arguments notwithstanding, studies also underscore that the relationship between pay and work motivation is more nuanced and complex than these linear arguments suggest – particularly when looking at pay rises tied to work performance. Bellé & Cantarelli (2015, p. 99), for instance, found that the effect of financial incentives on work motivation is 'negatively moderated by the intrinsic motivation of the participants, positively moderated by extrinsic motivation, and unaffected by public service motivation'. When individuals are intrinsically motivated to perform a job-related task, offering them economic incentives to enhance their productivity may thus backfire – as employees are putting effort into the task because they like the task itself, not for a monetary reward. By contrast, if employees are motivated by financial rewards, monetary rewards can strongly enhance work motivation. Whether higher pay enhances work motivation thus depends on whether employees are motivated by higher pay or by other motivators instead. The effect of pay-for-performance schemes also depends on how they are implemented. Andersen and Pallesen (2008), for instance, only find them to be effective where they are accompanied by good performance appraisal systems. Whether higher pay motivates hard work thus depends on what employees are motivated by in the first place and how pay decisions are made and tied to work effort. Perhaps unsurprisingly, then, a review of fifty-seven studies of pay for performance by Perry et al. (2009) finds that the average effects of monetary incentives on individual performance are rather small.

Next to pay, job design is a further immediate lever for managers to shape work motivation. Six job design factors have been paid particular attention to in the literature: goal setting, feedback, empowerment, teamwork, and, to a lesser extent, task motivation and task significance.

The link between goal setting and work motivation is theoretically developed in goal setting theory (Mitchell & Daniels, 2013). Intuitively, if public employees do not know what objectives they work towards – that is, if they have goal and role ambiguity – their commitment towards the organization, motivation to work hard and motivation to serve society suffers. Twenty-seven studies find such negative effects of goal ambiguity (five studies find null effects). Clear goals motivate employees in part through self-regulation: 'some employees perform better than others because they have different performance goals ... however, it is not the goals themselves but rather the discrepancies created by individuals' comparing how they perform to how they want to perform that motivate behaviour. The result of this evaluation is a sense of self-approval or self-dissatisfaction that serves to motivate individuals to act in ways that produce a positive self-evaluation or reduce a negative self-evaluation' (Wright, 2004, p. 60). A smaller number of studies shed light on other aspects of goal setting. Eight studies find that more challenging goals motivate more (though one finds the opposite). Overly challenging goals can, as noted, undermine motivation by undermining an employee's sense of self-efficacy. Three studies underscore that goals are more motivating when employees are committed to them; else, the aforementioned self-regulation is unlikely to be activated and motivating behaviour.

Related to goal setting is the importance of managerial feedback on employee goal attainment. Seventeen studies find a positive effect of feedback (five find a null effect). The quality and amount of feedback that employees receive thus matters for workplace motivation (Moynihan & Pandey, 2007; Paarlberg,

2007). To name a few, feedback from supervisors, service users and peers can reduce goal ambiguity for employees (Wright, 2004); help employees understand how their jobs create pro-social impact; and help employees understand where to improve to attain performance goals. Quality feedback can thus enhance motivation through a range of mechanisms.

Beyond that, job design studies have looked at job-level factors which empower employees – that is, factors which give employees a sense that they can contribute to deciding which objectives they need to tackle and how. Empowerment encompasses involvement in decision-making, job autonomy and responsibility, skill development, and an ability to express initiative (Petter et al., 2002). Factors associated with empowerment have overwhelmingly positive effects. Empowerment and participation in decision-making is found to have positive effects on work motivation and organizational commitment in twenty studies (five studies find no effect, and only a single study finds a negative effect). Moreover, job autonomy is found to have positive effects in four studies (with a null effect in two further studies). Job characteristics theory thus seems to hold its own in the public sector: public employees who sense that they have independence and control over their work tasks – and thus feel more responsible for work outcomes – are more motivated to work hard.

Related to empowerment, sixteen studies have identified positive effects of teamwork on work motivation and organizational commitment (two studies find null effects, and two find negative effects). Teamwork can enhance motivation through several motivators in our typology. It can enhance employees' sense of belonging and relatedness at work, thus making work more pleasurable (Medcof, 2006). It can enhance their identification with their work group, enhancing their motivation to work hard to achieve group goals (Medcof, 2006). Moreover, working in the presence of others can enhance social pressures – and thus incentives – to work hard, as team members can compare their effort and results among each other (Cornelissen, 2012).

3.4.4 Management-Level Determinants of Work Motivation

Management-level determinants look to attributes and behaviours of managers: what managerial actions and attributes enhance employee motivation? Public administration scholarship has focused on two leadership styles in particular: leader–member exchange and transformational leadership.

Thirty-five studies find positive effects of, broadly construed, leader–member exchange on work motivation/performance, PSM and organizational commitment (three find negative effects; six find null effects). Rooted in social

Table 5 Job-level determinants of work motivation

Antecedents	Work motivation			Individual performance			Intrinsic motivation			Public service motivation			Org. commit. & identification			TOTAL	
	Sig. +ive	Sig. -ive	Not sig	Sig. +ive	Sig. -ive	Not sig	Sig. +ive	Sig. -ive	Not sig	Sig. +ive	Sig. -ive	Not sig.	Sig. +ive	Sig. -ive	Not sig.	Freq.	%
Job-level variables																	
Tenure	3	7	2	2	1	2				8	1	26	9	10	17	88	6.69
Supervisory status	4	1	5	2	1	2				12	3	8	10	6	8	62	4.71
Salary/Bonuses	13	4	11	10	0	3				4	1	9	1	1	0	57	4.33
Goal/role ambiguity	0	14	2	0	1	0				0	5	2	0	7	1	32	2.43
Benefits (medical, pension, childcare, etc.)	9	3	3	4	0	2				7	0	4	7	0	4	32	2.43
Participation (empowerment)	12	0	0	1	0	0							7	1	5	26	1.98
Feedback	6	0	0	2	0	0				8	0	5	1	0	0	22	1.67
HR practices (support, fairness, etc.)	1	0	0				1	0	0	2	0	2	10	0	5	21	1.60
Teamwork	6	0	0	0	1	0							10	1	2	20	1.52
Job security	4	1	2	1	0	0							5	0	3	16	1.22
Training	8	0	2										3	0	2	15	1.14
Work ethic endorsement	1	0	0										10	0	3	14	1.06
Positive work environment	1	0	0	3	0	0				5	0	3	2	0	0	14	1.06

									Total	Frequency
Work hours	0	3	5				1	2	2	13	0.99
Job routineness	0	7	1				0	0	3	12	0.91
Goal/task difficulty	6	1	1				2	0	0	10	0.76
Task motivation (interesting task)	7	0	0				1	0	0	8	0.61
Task significance	5	0	1				1	0	0	7	0.53
Promotions	5	1	0				0	0	1	7	0.53
Resources	3	0	0	2	0	0	2	0	0	7	0.53
Teleworking	4	2	0							6	0.46
Job autonomy	3	0	0	1	0	1	0	0	1	6	0.46
Job enlargement	4	0	0				1	0	0	5	0.38
Job enrichment	5	0	0							5	0.38
Non-financial incentives	4	0	0							4	0.30
Job flexibility	1	0	2	0	0	1				4	0.30
Knaves (career, performance appraisal)	1	1	2							4	0.30
Knights (public values, benefit society)	2	0	1							3	0.23
Work pressure	0	0	2	0	0	1				3	0.23
Goal commitment	3	0	0							3	0.23
Job importance	2	0	0	1	0	1				2	0.15

Table 5 (cont.)

Antecedents	Work motivation Sig. +ive	Sig. -ive	Not sig	Individual performance Sig. +ive	Sig. -ive	Not sig	Intrinsic motivation Sig. +ive	Sig. -ive	Not sig	Public service motivation Sig. +ive	Sig. -ive	Not sig	Org. commit. & identification Sig. +ive	Sig. -ive	Not sig	TOTAL Freq.	%
Recess appointees	1	0	0	0	2	0										2	0.15
Beneficiary contact	0	2	0	0	0	1										2	0.15
Enhanced work demands																2	0.15
Merit pay							0	0	1				0	1	0	2	0.15
Emotional work				0	0	1										1	0.08
Lack of connection between responsibilities and org. goals	0	1	0	0	0	1										1	0.08
Perceived social impact	1	0	0	0	0	1										1	0.08
Low compliance burden	0	1	0													1	0.08
Absence/sickness	0	1	0													1	0.08

* Multiple classifications per study were possible. Percentages are the share of the total determinants tested. Number of times that statistically significant positive, negative and insignificant associations were found.

Source: Our own literature review and, with adaptations, Ritz et al. (2016).

exchange theory, Leader–Member Exchange (LMX) is a management practice that highlights the importance of the quality of the relationship between a leader and a follower (Graen & Uhl-Bien, 1995). When leaders and followers have a good relationship – which are often emotional relationships extending beyond the scope of employment – 'mechanisms of reciprocity and social exchange become effective: the leader and the employee trust each other, employees feel valued by their supervisor, and effective working relationships develop' (Tummers & Knies, 2013, pp. 3–4). Reciprocity, trust and feeling valued in turn can enhance the engagement and contribution of employees towards their team and organization – and thus work motivation and commitment. Several practices foment LMX, for instance: leaders demonstrating to employees that they support them and are there to help them develop their work and careers; and leaders providing insights to employees on how the organization works, thus fomenting trust and a perception among employees that they make a difference to the organization (cf., e.g., Hsieh, 2016; Buelens & Van den Broeck, 2007). Some studies suggest LMX is all the more important for older civil servants, who place greater value on working in a supportive environment; at the same time, LMX has positive average effects in a range of contexts, from Texas to Taipei, to name a few (Sabharwal, 2014; Chen, Lee & Chou, 2014).

Next to LMX, seven studies find positive evidence for a second leadership style: transformational leadership (with one study finding no effect). Transformational leaders create, communicate and instil a vision and sense of mission that helps employees transcend their own self-interests in favour of the organization's goals (Burns, 1978). In doing so, transformational leaders also clarify organizational goals, set challenging goals and, frequently, enhance the perception of employees that their jobs are interesting (Bronkhorst, Steijn & Vermeeren, 2015). The pro-social vision and mission of public sector organizations arguably lends itself in particular to transformational leadership efforts (Paarlberg & Lavigna, 2010). Transformational leadership is one of the few variables for which public administration research offers experimental – rather than mere correlational – evidence. In a field experiment with Italian nurses, Bellé (2013b) shows that nurses exposed to transformational leadership perform better. Bellé's (2013b) experiment also underscores the importance of interactions between factors in driving work motivation. The effect of transformational leadership is larger for employees who are brought into contact with beneficiaries of their work and for employees who are reminded through a self-persuasion intervention that they make a positive difference in people's lives. Transformational leadership thus may have a particularly positive effect where it is combined with job design interventions which reinforce the salience of the organization's positive contributions to society (though, of course, one can construe such job design interventions equally as transformational leadership practices).

A smaller set of studies has looked to a range of other management actions. This includes giving employees a sense of stability within the organization, enhancing commitment to the organization's mission and providing effective administrative and political coping. The evidence on these is limited, however (with one study supporting each) (see Table 6).

3.4.5 Organizational-Level Determinants of Work Motivation

A last strand of public administration scholarship has looked to characteristics of the organization as a whole to explain public sector work motivation. Three organizational characteristics have been studied in particular depth, with more than ten studies dedicated to each: red tape, person–organization fit and cooperative organizational cultures.

Red tape is the most studied organizational characteristic. Twenty-one studies associate it with lower work motivation, performance, PSM or organizational commitment (though five studies, remarkably, find a positive effect on, in particular, organizational commitment). Red tape – excessive levels of bureaucratic procedures which are redundant, time-consuming and/or hindering effective policies and management – can de-motivate public employees through several mechanisms. For instance, they can frustrate outcome-motivated public employees by hindering results achievement or their ability to help out service users (Stazyk, Pandey & Wright, 2011). Moreover, high compliance burdens to deliver results in the context of excessive regulations can require significant time and resource sacrifices by employees. Public employees who do not perceive any functionality in these regulations will be de-motivated by the sacrifices they need to make for them (Van Loon, 2017).

Person–organization fit (P–O fit) is the second most studied organizational antecedent. P–O fit variably refers to the congruency between patterns of organizational values and patterns of individual values (Chatman, 1989) or, more broadly, the extent to which employees have shared characteristics and views with the organization they work for. Eleven studies find a positive effect of P–O fit on performance and, in particular, organizational commitment (with one study each finding a negative and null effect). Theoretically, this positive effect is plausible. P–O fit can enhance performance and commitment by enhancing employee perceptions that their organization allows them to fulfil

Table 6 Management-level determinants of work motivation

Antecedents	Work motivation			Individual performance			Intrinsic motivation			Public service motivation			Org. commit. & identification			TOTAL	
	Sig. +ive	Sig. -ive	Not sig	Sig. +ive	Sig. -ive	Not sig	Sig. +ive	Sig. -ive	Not sig	Sig. +ive	Sig. -ive	Not sig	Sig. +ive	Sig. -ive	Not sig.	Freq.	%
Management-level variables																	
Leadership support (LMX)	4	0	0	6	0	0				9	3	0	13	0	6	41	3.12
Transformational lead.	1	0	0	3	0	1				3	0	0	3	0	0	11	0.84
Ethical leadership	1	0	0										1	0	1	2	0.15
Leadership stability	1	0	0										1	0	0	2	0.15
Leadership mission commitment	2	0	0													2	0.15
Leader's effective administration	1	0	0													1	0.08
Unskilled manager	0	1	0													1	0.08
Leader's relations oriented				1	0	0										1	0.08
Fair management	1	0	0													1	0.08
Appraisal accuracy	1	0	0													1	0.08
Manager's tenure							0	0	1							1	0.08
Manager's education							0	0	1							1	0.08
Self-persuasion interventions				1	0	0										1	0.08

* Multiple classifications per study were possible. Percentages are the share of the total determinants tested. Number of times statistically significant positive, neutral and negative associations with work motivation were found.

Source: Our own literature review. The data for Public Service Motivation has been adapted from Ritz et al. (2016).

their personal values and aspirations. It can also mediate the effect of other variables. Wright and Pandey (2008), for instance, show that when employees perceive that their values are aligned with those of their organizations, their PSM has a stronger effect on organizational commitment.

Related to value congruence and P–O fit, a third set of studies has looked to the effects of organizational cultures. Nine studies, in particular, have found that public employees in organizations with cooperative cultures are more committed, motivated to work hard and serve society, and perform (two studies find a null effect; one study finds a negative effect); and five further studies have found that employees in organizations emphasizing transparency and fairness are more motivated (with two null effects studies). Cooperative organizational cultures emphasize fairness, inclusion and supportive work environments. Employees who are treated fairly – for instance, in their performance appraisal – are found to reciprocate with greater work motivation (Kim & Rubianty, 2011). Effective procedural design thus matters for work motivation not only in terms of reducing red tape but also by enhancing an employee perception of fairness and transparency. The effect of such procedures, however, is at the same time contingent upon culture. Lack of a supportive organizational culture, for instance, is found to undermine the credibility employees attribute to procedures designed to enhance performance such as performance pay systems (Kellough & Lu, 1993). Moreover, inclusiveness of cooperative organizational cultures – that is, organizations embracing and valuing diverse workforces – is found to have positive effects, in particular on the affective commitment of employees towards the organization (Ashikali & Tanachia, 2015). A range of dimensions of cooperative and supportive organizational cultures in government are thus associated with more motivated and committed public sector workforces.

Red tape, person–organization fit and cooperative organizational cultures are, of course, far from the only organizational determinants of public sector work motivation. Table 7 lists a panoply of other factors which have been studied in a more select number of works. Mission valence – the attractiveness and salience of an organization's purpose or social contribution to an employee (Rainey & Steinbauer, 1999) – is positively associated with greater work motivation or performance in eight studies. A high-performing organization has positive effects on employees in five studies; and good facilities matter positively in three studies (though another three find no effect).

The evidence an all remaining factors is limited; none have invariably positive or negative effects in more than two studies. A range of organizational-level factors which plausibly shape work motivation in public sectors around the world are thus altogether understudied. To name a few, this includes the

Table 7 Organizational-level determinants of work motivation

Antecedents	Work motivation			Individual performance			Intrinsic motivation			Public service motivation			Org. commit. & identification			TOTAL	
	Sig. +ive	Sig. -ive	Not sig	Sig. +ive	Sig. -ive	Not sig	Sig. +ive	Sig. -ive	Not sig	Sig. +ive	Sig. -ive	Not sig.	Sig. +ive	Sig. -ive	Not sig.	Freq.	%
Organizational-level variables																	
Red tape	1	14	2	0	1	0				0	1	2	4	5	2	32	2.43
Person–organization fit		0	0	2	0	0							9	1	1	13	0.99
Cooperative culture	2	0	0	1	0	0				1	0	2	5	1	0	12	0.91
Mission valence	4	0	0	4	0	0										8	0.61
Transparency/fairness	5	0	0	0	0	2										7	0.53
Good facilities	1	0	1	2	0	2										6	0.46
Org. performance	1	0	0	1	0	0	0	0	1				3	0	0	6	0.46
Size of workplace	0	1	0				0	0	1				3	0	1	6	0.46
User orientation	1	0	1													2	0.15
Org. reforms													1	1	2	4	0.30
Budget				2	0	1										3	0.23
Org. goal conflict	0	0	1	0	1	0										2	0.15
Weberian bureaucracy				1	1	0										2	0.15
Working sector													0	0	2	2	0.15
Representative bureaucracy				1	1	0										2	0.15
Results-oriented				1	0	0										1	0.08
Supportive stakeholders	1	0	0													1	0.08

Table 7 (cont.)

Antecedents	Work motivation			Individual performance			Intrinsic motivation			Public service motivation			Org. commit. & identification			TOTAL	
	Sig. +ive	Sig. -ive	Not sig	Sig. +ive	Sig. -ive	Not sig	Sig. +ive	Sig. -ive	Not sig	Sig. +ive	Sig. -ive	Not sig	Sig. +ive	Sig. -ive	Not sig	Freq.	%
Quality of political exeactives	0	1	0													1	0.08
Bureaucrats input into policy				1	0	0										1	0.08
Org. flexibility				1	0	0										1	0.08
Skills (human capital such as IT competencies)				1	0	0										1	0.08
Staffing (recruitment, workload spreads)				1	0	0										1	0.08
Org. complexity													1	0	0	1	0.08
Political sensitivity													1	0	0	1	0.08
Communication with employees													1	0	0	1	0.08
Value alignment	1	0	0													1	0.08
Org. reputation	1	0	0							4	0	2	0	1	0	7	0.53
Perception of org. politics													0	1	0	1	0.08
Other																53	4.03
Total																1316	100

* Multiple classifications per study were possible. Percentages are the share of the total determinants tested. Number of times statistically significant positive, neutral and negative associations with work motivation were found.

Source: Our own literature review. The data for Public Service Motivation has been adapted from Ritz et al. (2016).

effects of different social norms of organizations (for instance, regarding a differential acceptability of corruption and unethical behaviour); different organizational structures (for instance, flat versus more hierarchical organizations); and different organizational human resource management practices (for instance, different recruitment practices). As this list underscores, many of the more actionable practices for organizations to enhance work motivation are thus also precisely the ones that public administration scholars have neglected to study.

3.5 Conclusions

Overall, the 'what' and 'how' of public administration research on public sector work motivation suggests that public administration studies have paid much more attention to extrinsic and other-regarding motivators – in particular, PSM and organizational commitment – than to intrinsic and self-regarding motivators; that we know much more about public sector work motivation in the West – and, in particular, the United States – than about the developing world; that what we know comes principally from partial correlations in observational studies – a problematic basis for *causal* inferences about the determinants of work motivation; and that comparisons of findings have to be taken with a grain of salt as different studies use different measurements of work motivation – there is no generally accepted measurement scale.

With those caveats in mind: what, if anything, can be learned from our review of public administration studies on the determinants of public sector work motivation? Several lessons stand out.

To begin with, our review suggests that the determinants of public sector work motivation are invariably complex. Factors at the individual, job, management and organizational level are all found to significantly affect the work motivation – and individual motivators – of public employees. Moreover, factors across levels interact. To illustrate, the effect of leadership styles (such as transformational leadership) varies depending on how jobs are designed (for instance, depending on the extent to which jobs link employees with beneficiaries of their work). This complexity in factors and interactions underscores that there are no silver bullets in public sector workforce motivation. Public sector employees will be motivated or not as a function of the joint effect of a range of individual, job, management and organizational-level factors. This finding cautions against monocausal explanations and single-practice interventions as holy grails for workforce motivation. Some generalizations about which factors *tend* to matter more than others are nonetheless possible.

At the individual level, the review underscores that demographic factors do not have consistent effects. Gender, age, education and other demographics are not clear-cut determinants of work motivation in public sectors. By contrast, attitudes, values and traits at the individual-level have more consistent effects. Satisfaction with one's job and organization; trust in management; and a sense of self-efficacy are particularly consistent determinants of greater work motivation. Managers thus need to assess how their interventions affect not only work motivation directly but also other attitudes and values of public servants – such as trust in management – which affect their motivation.

Job-level determinants offer more direct levers for managers to enhance work motivation. Higher pay and benefits matter for attracting and retaining motivated staff and enhancing their commitment. Pay-for-performance, by contrast, has mixed effects – it is more likely to work where employees value financial incentives and performance appraisals are implemented well. Job design similarly matters. Clear and challenging goals, quality feedback, job autonomy, participation in decision-making, teamwork and less routine tasks are all associated with greater work motivation. Lastly, HRM practices matter, with evidence for positive effects of training and job security (by contrast, organizational tenure is largely insignificant).

At the management level, public administration studies underscore the importance of leader–member exchange and transformational leadership for public sector work motivation. At the organizational level, public administration evidence is strongest on the importance of cutting red tape, enhancing person-organization fit and strengthening cooperative organizational cultures, which emphasize fairness, inclusion and supportive work environments.

In short, public administration scholarship emphasizes the importance of satisfaction, trust and self-efficacy at the individual level; pay, job design and (select) human resource management practices at the job level; transformational leadership and leader–member exchange at the management level; and cutting excessive procedures, creating cooperative cultures and strengthening P–O fit at the organizational level.

At the same time, it leaves a range of other determinants under- or only superficially studied. Non-pecuniary self-interested incentives (epitomized by 'employee of the month' awards) and practices to make work fun (epitomized by ping-pong tables in Google offices), for instance, have been hardly studied; practices such as teamwork are often treated as a dichotomous explanators – while their complexities, of course, would merit book-length treatments. Public administration research on public sector work motivation thus appears unbalanced in both the motivators it studies and the underlying motivational practices.

With this caveat in mind, we turn in our final section from reviewing determinants to reviewing lessons for management practice: What can we learn from public administration works about motivating public employees in practice? And what lessons do other disciplines offer which are currently neglected in public administration research?

4 The Art of Motivating Public Employees in Practice: Lessons from and for Public Administration Research

What can we learn from scholarly works about motivating public employees in practice? We address this question in two steps. Based on our systematic literature review, we, first, review lessons for practice from public administration scholarship. We focus on major lessons – that is, lessons which at least five studies have referred to. The review will lay out several lessons for practice *and* gaps in lessons for practice. On several motivators in our typology – in particular, non-pecuniary incentives, relatedness, task enjoyment and warm glow – public administration scholarship provides fewer insights to practitioners. In a second step, we thus draw selectively on lessons from studies in other disciplines – in particular, economics, psychology and business studies – to both flag lessons for practitioners for these remaining motivators and underscore missing areas of research in public administration scholarship.[15] To enable meaningful insights for practitioners, we discuss each lesson with an illustrative example which showcases how the lesson works in practice.

One important caveat is due. Our literature review revealed that the inferences scholars draw for practice do not always map onto their findings about the determinants of public sector work motivation. For instance, while a large number of studies underscore the importance of pay for attracting and retaining motivated staff, pay levels rarely feature in recommendations for practice by scholars. Readers interested in practitioner implications may thus wish to read this section in conjunction with the conclusion of Section 3.5 for a more complete understanding of the explicit *and* implicit lessons for practice from public administration research.

4.1 Lessons from Public Administration Scholarship

Lesson 1 Ensure that human resource management practices – including recruitment, pay, training and job design – foster public service motivation

Underlying motivator(s): PSM, plus organizational commitment and intrinsic enjoyment
Starting in 1987, one of Brazil's then-poorest regions – Ceara – hired 7,300 health workers to provide preventive health care to young families, including

---

[17] Given the magnitude of this literature in other disciplines, we, by necessity, limit ourselves to drawing on selective insights.

vaccinations, prenatal care and oral rehydration. On the face of it, the programme was a control nightmare: unskilled workers, spread across the countryside over a territory the size of France, were seemingly poorly incentivized, being paid minimum wages on temporary contracts. Shirking and moonlighting of workers was thus a natural expectation. Yet, the opposite occurred. Health workers visited 850,000 families every month (65 per cent of the state's population) and went above and beyond their job description, starting – for instance – health campaigns in their communities. The programme ended up winning Latin America's first UNICEF prize for child support programs. Why did hardly supervised temporary unskilled health workers on a limited pay in a region replete with poverty go above and beyond? One answer lies in how the programme staged the hiring process of workers to foster public service motivation. Workers were hired in town events with both individual interviews and group meetings. In these meetings – on which local citizens frequently eavesdropped – the state selection committee repeatedly told applicants that 'this program is yours, and it is you who will determine its success ... [Y]our community does not have to lose so many of its babies'. They also signalled to applicants that being hired is an 'honour' which 'had proven their commitment to the community' (Tendler & Freedheim, 1994, p. 1777). In front of their whole communities, employees were thus socialized in public hiring events into PSM and public service prestige, motivating them to work hard for their communities.

This example underscores the first – and most frequently mentioned – lesson from public administration research about how to enhance work motivation in the public sector: ensure that human resource management practices foster public service motivation. The foremost recommendation (fifty-nine studies) is to ensure that public sector organizations attract and select candidates to the public sector with high public service motivation. This is followed by generic recommendations to incorporate PSM in human resource management practices (thirty-two studies); recommendations to rely on traditional – rather than performance-related – pay schemes to avoid crowding out PSM (thirty studies); recommendations to train employees in public service values and, more generally, create public service-oriented organizational cultures (eighteen studies each); recommendations to design jobs for public service-motivated employees (thirteen studies), including – in particular – enabling (street-level) bureaucrats to meet with beneficiaries of their work (twelve studies).

These recommendations are intuitive: individuals who are motivated to serve the public – because of selection, training or job design, for instance – are more motivated to work hard in the public sector. They are also aligned with the typology we developed in Section 2. More importantly, they matter for practice: PSM often does not feature prominently in public sector human resource management practices, such as how governments recruit staff (Christensen et al., 2017).

While this lesson matters for practice, unfortunately, public administration research remains often vague about *how* public sector organizations can effectively incorporate PSM into human resource management practice. Robust evidence for *how* public sector organizations can effectively select candidates with high PSM, for instance, is largely missing. To attract high PSM applicants, organizations may project public service-oriented missions and images and advertise job descriptions which make these public service missions salient to applicants. In fact, eleven studies recommend stressing public service values in human resource marking and branding. As in the Ceara example, they may, of course, also seek more creative ways to attract and socialize candidates into PSM (Tendler & Freedheim, 1994). To select high PSM applicants in turn, organizations may score resumes based on PSM – for instance, by gauging extracurricular behaviour – and inquire in interviews about PSM-related critical incidents; they may try to also 'select out' low PSM applicants by trying to provide a realistic portrayal of the job and its public service nature in interviews (Christensen et al., 2017). Hard evidence that any of these practices are effective is limited, however. In a recent field experiment with the police in the United States, for instance, Linos (2018) found that job advertisements which emphasize PSM are *not* effective at attracting high PSM applicants – plausibly as prospective applicants are already aware of the public service-oriented nature of public sector jobs. Public administration scholarship thus provides stronger evidence on the importance of incorporating PSM into human resource management practices than on *how* organizations can do so effectively.

The same conclusion applies, with two important caveats, to other HRM practices as well. Robust evidence on how to train public servants to enhance their public service values or how to create high PSM organizational cultures, for instance, is largely lacking. Public administration scholarship is somewhat more explicit on pay: eschew pay-for-performance in favour of traditional or alternative reward systems. As noted in Section 3, however, empirical evidence on this lesson is more nuanced and pointing to trade-offs. Pay-for-performance may, for instance, curb PSM but nonetheless enhance overall work motivation where the increase in motivation from self-interested incentives outweighs the decrease in motivation from a reduction in PSM.

Lastly, job design is, perhaps, the practice for which public administration scholarship – building on findings in other disciplines (Grant, 2008) –

provides the most specific insights for practitioners. In a field experiment with nurses in a public hospital in Italy, Bellé (2013a) shows that nurses brought in contact with beneficiaries of their work are more motivated to work hard. This puts a premium on job designs which connect employees to their pro-social impact – and thus enhance the significance and meaningfulness employees attribute to their contribution to society. Public sector organizations would thus do well to identify beneficiaries of specific programmes or jobs and create opportunities for direct contact and channels of feedback between employees and beneficiaries – provided, of course, such employee–beneficiary relations may be expected to be positive (see Table 8).[16]

Table 8 Human resource management practices to foster PSM

Managerial action	Freq.
Consider a candidate's public service motivation in selection decisions	62
Use public service motivation-specific management practices	32
Eschew pay for performance in favour of traditional or alternative reward systems[17]	30
Create public service-oriented organizational cultures	18
Train staff in public service values	18
Design jobs for public service-motivated individuals and assign them to such jobs	15
Incorporate contact with beneficiaries in job design of street-level bureaucrats	13
Stress public service values in human resources marketing and branding	11[*]
Inform job applicants about organizational culture, so they can assess a fit with their personal values	1
Assess compatibility of applicant beliefs and values with organization before hiring	1

* Multiple classifications per study were possible.
Sources: Our own review and Ritz et al. (2016).

---

[16] 'Beneficiary' contact with, for instance, tax frauds for tax officials or neighbourhoods disdaining the police for police officers may, of course, backfire and reduce PSM instead.

[17] As a caveat, ten studies also recommend implementing, in the broadest sense, NPM reforms to enhance PSM. Such reforms tend to comprise pay-for-performance schemes.

Lesson 2 Define and communicate a clear mission for your organization, set individual goals and tasks related to this mission, and show employees how their goals and tasks help mission attainment

Underlying motivator(s): organizational commitment, plus PSM and intrinsic enjoyment

In 1961, President Kennedy gave the US National Aeronautics and Space Administration (NASA) one overarching mission: to put a man on the moon and return him safely to Earth before the end of the 1960s. When he visited NASA headquarters that year for the first time, he met a janitor who was mopping the floor late in the day. When asking him what was he doing mopping the floors so late, the employee replied that he was working late because he was helping to put a man on the moon. What NASA had thus achieved was that, down to the lowest levels of the organizational echelon, members of the organization understood the mission of their organization and how their own job tasks helped the organization attain it (Carton, 2018). The resulting greater commitment to their organization (and its goal to put a man on the moon), motivation to serve society (to put a man on the moon) and, potentially, intrinsic enjoyment (due to a greater sense of achievement) can all motivate employees to work harder.

This example illustrates the second lesson from public administration research for practice: define and communicate a clear mission for your organization, set individual goals and tasks related to this mission, and show employees how their goals and tasks help mission attainment. These sets of practices are, of course, central to transformational leadership. As noted in Section 3, transformational leaders create, communicate and instil a vision and sense of mission that helps employees transcend their own self-interests in favour of the organization's goals (Burns, 1978). In line with this reasoning, thirteen studies recommend the adoption of transformational leadership practices more generally. Other studies, instead, recommend specific practices associated with our overarching lesson – these being, sequentially: defining a clear and meaningful organizational mission (four studies recommend this practice); communicating this mission to your employees (twenty-seven studies emphasize the importance of communication); disaggregating this mission into a set of organizational goals and, based on these goals, setting clear individuals goals for employees linked to these organizational goals and mission (seven studies); thereby ensuring that these goals are specific and challenging but attainable (six studies); and, lastly, assigning job tasks which are both challenging and clearly linked to these goals (four studies).

Table 9 Managerial actions to define and communicate mission, goals and tasks for organization and employees

Managerial action	Freq.
Use communication to clarify goals, show how employees can benefit society and highlight organizational fit with the employee	27
Use transformational leadership	13
Set specific and doable but challenging job goals, linked to organizational goals	7
Define and communicate clear roles and goals	6
Assign variety of specific, clear and challenging tasks to employees	5
Set a clear, legitimate, important and feasible organizational mission to be able to align employee duties and values with mission	4

* Multiple classifications per study were possible.
Sources: Our own review and Ritz et al. (2016).

As a result of these steps – and coming back to the NASA example – 'when this connection [referring to the connection between employee tasks and organizational objectives] was strongest, employees construed their day-to-day work not as short-term tasks ("I'm building electrical circuits") but as the pursuit of NASA's long-term objective ("I'm putting a man on the moon") and the aspiration this objective symbolized ("I'm advancing science")' (Carton, 2018).

In public sectors with vague, conflicting and multiple goals, following this recommendation is, of course, easier said than done. The evidence does suggest that it is worthwhile trying, however (see Table 9).

Lesson 3 Provide feedback to employees on 1) performance, 2) opportunities for learning and 3) impact on beneficiaries

Underlying motivator(s): incentives, organizational commitment, PSM and intrinsic enjoyment
Despite being far from the richest area globally, Shanghai has, for several years, topped global rankings for educational attainment in reading, mathematics and science. Observers attribute this outcome in part to the 'Shanghai secrets': a meticulous focus on instructional excellence (World Bank, 2016). One important part of these secrets is constant feedback to help teachers improve. In weekly meetings with mentor teachers, teachers look at how to overcome challenges and improve on their teaching. Moreover, senior teachers frequently – often twenty to thirty times a year – observe junior teachers' lessons to provide feedback. On top, teachers teaching the same subject

observe each other to provide peer feedback (World Bank, 2016). As a result, teachers face both subtle evaluation pressures to improve and, more importantly, constant learning opportunities. This quest for teaching quality has, within a few decades, dramatically improved instructional excellence and student outcomes.

As this example illustrates, feedback can be a powerful tool for organizations to motivate employees in multiple ways. Most obviously, managers – and even peers, as in the Shanghai examples – can use feedback to indicate to employees the extent to which they are meeting or exceeding objectives. In our review of public administration studies, twelve studies explicitly recommend such performance feedback. When providing such feedback, managers should holistically cover the range of goals an employee is to achieve. When managers provide feedback on some goals but not others, employees have been found to improve their performance only on those goals for which feedback has been provided (Locke & Latham, 2002). Feedback can, of course, also enable employees to learn how to improve and grow in their skills and career – thus enhancing their sense of competence, commitment to the organization and intrinsic enjoyment of work. Twelve studies explicitly link feedback to supportive management or enabling leadership. In line with the previous two lessons, feedback can, lastly, also help employees understand their (positive) impact on users and society – thus potentially enhance PSM.

While feedback thus matters for a range of motivators in the public sector, it is not without challenges in the public sector. The aforementioned vague goals complicate numeric feedback on goal attainment. As the Shanghai example illustrates, however, it is far from infeasible. Public sector managers may focus their feedback on qualitative judgements about progress, for instance, together with granular assessments about how well employees are developing their tasks, how their work is impacting others and what they could do to improve further (see Table 10).

Table 10 Managerial actions to increase feedback towards employees

Managerial action	Freq.
Provide feedback on performance	12
Provide feedback as part of a supportive management philosophy	12
Provide feedback on how employees' work benefits users	2

* Multiple classifications per study were possible.
Sources: Our own review and Ritz et al. (2016).

Lesson 4 Empower employees by enhancing job autonomy and participation in organizational decision-making

Underlying motivator(s): incentives, organizational commitment, PSM and intrinsic enjoyment

When Beethoven, Mozart and other classical composers wrote their pieces, they sometimes left blank spaces in their scores. In these so-called cadenzas, they gave soloists autonomy to play and improvise as they please for part of the piece. With the passage of time, other composers started to fill in these gaps, and orchestras instructed their soloists to follow these scripted cadenzas instead of their own improvisation. As a result, orchestras and conductors gained greater control over the concert experience. At the same time, however, they deprived soloists of the arguably most important moment in a concert to express themselves and shape their orchestra's musical output – or, in other words, of potentially one of the most motivating aspects of their jobs. Orchestras are becoming increasingly cognizant of this and are going back to the roots to empower soloists to improvise as they please (Kramer, 1991; The *Telegraph, 2015*).

As this example underscores, empowering employees can be a powerful motivator, and this is the fourth broad lesson drawn in public administration studies. As detailed in Section 3, empowerment is an umbrella concept which encompasses involvement in decision-making, job autonomy and responsibility, skill development, and an ability to express initiative (Petter et al., 2002). Thirteen studies explicitly recommend promoting employee participation in either organizational decision-making as a whole or the setting of goals and strategies more particularly. Four studies recommend enhancing employees' job autonomy – that is, greater freedom and discretion over work method (procedures and methods of one's work), work scheduling (sequencing and timing of tasks), and, at times, even work criteria (indicators/standards used to gauge quality of work) (cf. Breaugh, 1985). Lastly, three studies explicitly refer to empowerment through skill development and coaching for performance – for instance, through leadership assignments.

While empowerment can thus powerfully shape motivation, it is often not easy to implement in public sectors. Job autonomy runs counter to requirements for procedural controls in public sector organizations. Employee participation in organizational decision-making in turn runs counter to traditional top-down hierarchical organizational structures. Managerial resistance to employee empowerment can also come from legitimate concerns with unintended consequences in contexts in which employee goals diverge from organizational goals. Greater autonomy for corrupt employees might, for instance, motivate

Table 11 Managerial actions to empower employees

Managerial action	Freq.
Promote employee participation in organizational decision-making	8
Promote employee participation in setting goals and standards	5
Enhance employee job autonomy	4
Create opportunities for advancement and skill development through, e.g., leadership placements and opportunities to share opinions	3

* Multiple classifications per study were possible.
Sources: Our own review and Ritz et al. (2016).

them to work hard towards private enrichment. Similarly, shared strategic decision-making might lead to courses of action which prioritize employee welfare over organizational goals. Employee empowerment may thus intuitively require concurrent or prior managerial actions to enhance PSM and organizational commitment in employees to avoid backfiring (see lessons 1 and 2). Public administration scholarship is largely mute on – and thus unable to provide guidance – these nuances (see Table 11).

Lesson 5 Ensure that rules and procedures are effective and have a clear
  purpose which employees are aware of

Underlying motivator(s): intrinsic enjoyment, organizational commitment, PSM

Police officers join the police to fight crime. In many jurisdictions, however, they – in fact – spend little time on that. One UK government report finds that one-third of the time of police officers is spent on excessive bureaucracy. To cite just a few examples: nine officers have to supervise when a student constable investigates a burglary. If officers need to watch a suspect through a window, they need to fill out a 16-page form. And whenever officers make arrests, they need to enter the suspect's details in four or more separate databases (*The Telegraph*, 2010). This level of red tape impairs police work, which 'had become risk-averse, record keeping too elaborate and officers had been put in a position where their roles were too rigid to respond – particularly to pleas for help from the public'. Unable to help citizens in need and spending significant time on paperwork, police officers become increasingly de-motivated. Some local police forces have responded by drastically cutting red tape. The Staffordshire police, for instance, gave much greater discretion – and fewer rules – to police officers dealing with anti-social behaviour. Rather than having to write detailed reports which were then sent on to court, police officers were granted discretion to judge cases themselves. The result was a happier and more motivated workforce and a rise in the level of confidence in the police service by the general public (*The Guardian*, 2009).

As this example illustrates, and as detailed in Section 3, red tape – excessive levels of bureaucratic procedures which are redundant, time-consuming and/or hindering effective policies and management – can de-motivate public employees by hindering results achievement and requiring employees to make significant time and resource sacrifices to ensure compliance. Seven public administration studies thus explicitly recommend cutting red tape or clarifying rules which are perceived as unfair by public employees.

Note, though, that reducing red tape can, but need not, mean fewer rules. Rather, it means designing rules that are helpful – or what DeHart-Davis (2009a) calls green tape. Green tape means written rules which help attain desired outcomes (that is, they have valid means–ends relationships), employ optimal control (correctly balancing control and discretion), are consistently applied and have purposes which are clearly understood by employees. Green tape can motivate employees by enhancing perceived 'accountability and legitimate authority (promoted by written rules), the wise use of public resources (advanced by valid relationships between rule means and ends), managerial efficiency (facilitated by optimal control), fairness in the distribution of public resources (assisted by consistent rule application), and transparency (furthered by stakeholder understanding of rule purposes)' (DeHart-Davis, 2009a, p. 376).

In line with this logic, employees are more prone to follow 'green tape' rules (DeHart-Davis, 2009b) and more satisfied with their jobs in organizations with green tape rules (DeHart-Davis, Davis & Mohr, 2015). Motivating public employees thus does not require cutting rules. Rather, it requires managers to design rules that help employees undertake their jobs and, ultimately, the organization achieve its goals (see Table 12).

Table 12 Managerial actions to enhance the use of rules and procedures

Managerial action	Freq.
Reduce red tape	4
Enhance perceived fairness of organization by clarifying rules and procedures, including in appraisal systems	3

* Multiple classifications per study were possible.
Sources: Our own review and Ritz et al. (2016).

Lesson 6 Promote a supportive work environment and culture

Underlying motivator(s): organizational commitment, intrinsic enjoyment and relatedness

In any US Marine base, something curious happens in the lunch canteen: Marines line up in rank order to get food. This rank order, however, is reversed. The most junior Marines eat first; the most senior officials eat last. No rule or command imposes this. Rather, it is part of the Marines' culture. The welfare of the marines comes first. This matters as much in the canteen hall as on the battlefield: no man is left behind (Sinek, 2017).

Creating such supportive work environments which emphasize employee welfare is the final major lesson from public administration research. Eight studies recommend supportive work environments generally. Others recommend more specific management practices, including training programmes which recognize growth needs of staff (fifteen studies); work–life balance and family-friendly policies (seven studies); the promotion of supportive relationships and friendships among employees (three studies); and, lastly, treating employees with respect (two studies) and managing diversity (one study). A diverse range of managerial actions can thus foster supportive work environments, which can enhance employees' feelings of safety and relatedness, affective commitment to the organization and intrinsic enjoyment of work (see Table 13).

In sum, our review of recommendations from public administration scholarship underscores the importance of incorporating PSM in HRM decisions; defining, communicating and aligning clear organizational and individual goals; providing feedback; empowering employees; designing effective rules with a clearly communicated purpose; and promoting a supportive work environment.

Table 13 Managerial actions to promote a supportive work environment and culture

Managerial action	Freq.
Offer training programmes	15
Create a supportive work environment	8
Promote work–life balance and family-friendly policies	7
Foster supportive relationships and friendships among employees	3
Treat employees with respect and dignity	2
Promote diversity management	1

* Multiple classifications per study were possible.
Sources: Our own review and Ritz et al. (2016).

At the same time, public administration scholarship is virtually mute on lessons for practitioners on four other motivators in our typology: warm glow, relatedness at work, non-pecuniary incentives and, to a lesser extent, task enjoyment. In the next section, we draw selectively on illustrative examples from other disciplines – in particular, economics, organizational psychology and business studies – to demonstrate to public administration scholars that these neglected motivators are well worth studying. As a collateral benefit, this Element can thus also provide more holistic guidance to practitioners seeking to motivate public employees.

4.2 Lessons from Other Disciplines for Practitioners and Public Administration Scholars

To showcase the utility of studying practices to enhance the four neglected motivators in our typology – warm glow, relatedness at work, self-interested non-financial incentives and task enjoyment – we present in this last section a lesson on and illustrative example of each. Readers interested in more detail about practices to enhance these neglected motivators are encouraged to consult the cited references.

Lesson 7: Make work (more) fun

Underlying motivator(s): enjoyment
When Andrei Geim and Kostya Novoselov received the joint Nobel prize in physics in 2010, the Nobel Committee emphasized something rather peculiar: how playing in their laboratory at the University of Manchester had enabled the two to make their ground-breaking discovery of graphene. That play enabled this ground-breaking discovery was no coincidence. Their laboratory had an explicit policy to allow researchers to experiment with fun and crazy ideas on Friday evenings in a playful way. What started as a scheme to increase motivation and reduce stress ended up providing the scientific grounds for a Nobel prize (*The Independent, 2013*).

Task enjoyment – including having fun at work – is, as we had argued in our typology, an important motivator. It gives employees positive affective emotions – that is, a feeling of pleasure – which in turn makes employees willing to spend more time at work, work with greater intensity, judge work more favourably and take on more challenging objectives (Wegener & Petty, 1996). Hence, managers should design jobs and organizations in ways that enable employees to have (some) fun at work – which, of course, is more challenging for some tasks than others (Isen, 2000). A large literature in organizational psychology, management and economics has studied the manifold ways through which organizations and managers can make work (more) fun (see, for example, Seo, Barret & Bartunek, 2004).

By contrast, public administration scholarship has been largely mute on what public sector organizations can do to make work in government organizations more fun. It would do well to fill this void.

Lesson 8 Carefully design self-interested non-pecuniary incentives

Underlying motivator(s): incentives
In World War II, the German Air Force sought to incentivize fighter pilots through both league tables of victories for each pilot and a daily bulletin which recognized spectacular accomplishments (such as a very high number of enemy ships sunk). These accomplishments were broadcast publicly through the radio and press through the German territory and thus provided pilots with a short-term elevation of their status in the eyes of others (though nothing more tangible). How did fighter pilots react to this combination of public recognition of high performance and status competition between pilots? A recent paper in economics finds that the best pilots tried harder, scored more and died no more frequently when their peers were publicly recognized. By contrast, public recognition of peers led average pilots to score few additional victories yet – due to greater risk-taking – die at a significantly higher rate. In conjunction, status competition and public recognition may have thus reduced the German Air Force's overall effectiveness (Ager, Bursztyn & Voth, 2016).

As this example of 'killer incentives' illustrates, non-pecuniary but self-interested incentives – such as status competition, peer pressure and recognition – can shape the motivation of employees in powerful and complex ways. 'Employee-of-the-month' awards, Air Force bulletins or halls of fame in sports are, among many other examples, symbolic rewards which build on a human need for approbation to motivate effort. A large literature in economics and organizational psychology has studied these and other self-regarding non-pecuniary rewards (e.g. Ashraf, Bandiera & Jack, 2014; Chan, Frey, Gallus & Torgler, 2014; Kosfeld & Neckermann, 2011). Their findings underscore the complex effects of non-pecuniary rewards. Some studies, for instance, find that work performance suffers as a result of direct rankings and explicit comparisons with others in the group (e.g. Ashraf, Bandiera & Lee, 2014). As Winston Churchill put it for the example of recognition, "[a] medal glitters, but it also casts a shadow" (cited in Knowles, 2014, p. 215). Others associate non-pecuniary rewards with greater effort (e.g. Chan et al., 2014; Kosfeld & Neckermann, 2011).

Studying the complex effects of such non-pecuniary, self-interested incentives in public sectors is thus well warranted – not least as they offer a potentially cost-effective means of motivating staff in times of budget crises. As evidenced, however, they may also backfire. Public administration scholarship to date, however, provides little guidance on these nuances of non-pecuniary rewards.

Lesson 9 Make your employees feel good about their pro-social impact

Underlying motivator(s): warm glow

'Feel good about yourself – Give blood!' reads an advertisement of the American Red Cross (cited in Andreoni, 1990). This feeling is arguably well warranted. Donating a unit of blood can save up to three lives. Yet, fewer than 5 per cent of Europe's eligible population donates (Costa-Font, Jofre-Bonet & Yen, 2013). Donating blood is thus a pro-social act: donors incur personal costs for a collective benefit. It is, however, also an act of 'impure altruism': donors receive moral satisfaction from donating. That this is so is evidenced in a range of studies. Donors with O-negative blood – most pro-socially valuable, as it is compatible with all blood types – do not donate more than others, for instance (Wildman & Hollingsworth, 2009). If blood donations were motivated by pure altruistic concerns for the welfare of others, O-negative donors should arguably donate more. The American Red Cross ad directly builds on this moral satisfaction motivation – or what we termed 'warm glow' in our typology – to attract donations (cf. Andreoni, 1990).

This 'warm glow' motivator has seen – building on Andreoni's (1990) classic article with almost 5,000 citations – recurrent application to workplace motivation in studies in economics and psychology. By contrast, public administration scholarship has been largely mute on how to enhance 'warm glow' motivation of public employees. This is a relevant omission from both a practitioner and an academic perspective. As 'warm glow' may correlate with PSM, it might bias inferences in PSM studies which do not control for it. Future public administration work may thus wish to pay greater attention to disentangling working hard to help others from working hard to feel good about helping others.

Lesson 10 Make your team members care about each other

Underlying motivator(s): relatedness

When Pep Guardiola took over as coach of FC Barcelona in 2008, he joined a football team which had had limited success in previous years. Four years later, when Guardiola left, the opposite was true: Barça won 14 titles in four years, including two Champions League wins to make Barcelona the top team in Europe. Guardiola thus became the most successful coach in football's recent history. Among many management practices which spurred this success, Guardiola was renowned for the relatedness and affective bonds he created within his team. One particular measure that he took was to oblige all players and staff members to have lunch together every single working day. By doing so, he helped strengthen personal relations among all players and staff members, building their friendships and enjoying each other's company. It paid off handsomely in performances on the pitch (*The Telegraph, 2012*).

How to strengthen relatedness – lasting emotional connections and feelings of care between team members which make work more pleasurable – has seen a large number of studies in organizational psychology (see, among many, Pavey, Greitemeyer & Sparks, 2012). These underscore that managers can foster relatedness by implementing social activities that break down the organization's hierarchy and communication barriers among employees, allowing them to get to know each other at a deeper, more personal level. As a result, employees feel psychologically safer at work, feeling more comfortable to share their emotions and feelings without fear (Edmonson, 1999). Next to reducing negative affect (such as fear and stress), relatedness also motivates through positive affect: stimulation from interpersonal closeness and communion. With organizations – including in the public sector – relying more and more on teamwork to reach their objectives, managerial practices to strengthen relatedness arguably become ever more important (Cross, Rebele & Grant, 2016). Yet, public administration scholarship has little to say about them to date. It would thus do well to expand research on this final motivator in our typology.

4.3 Towards a More Holistic, Actionable and Robust Study of Public Sector Work Motivation in Public Administration

Motivating public employees is invariably complex. As our typology underscores, employees may be motivated for other- or self-regarding reasons and by the outcomes of their work and the work itself. Our review of public administration studies underscores the panoply of individual-, job-, management- and organizational-level factors which interact to shape these sources of motivation. Of the many determinants and practices that shape public sector work motivation, public administration has paid relatively more attention to practices shaping PSM, organizational commitment and financial incentives. To build a more holistic understanding of public sector work motivation, public administration scholars would do well to study with equal fervour other potential motivators: non-pecuniary rewards, task enjoyment, relatedness and warm glow. This holds all the more as these motivators are likely to gain in prominence in the future of the public sector workplace – with concurrent austerity pressures and greater market demand for highly skilled employees enhancing retention and motivation challenges.

To provide guidance to practitioners, public administration scholars would also do well to move from the study of more abstract variables to assessing specific, actionable practices. Many recommendations in public administration scholarship run the risk of being perceived as trivial and overly generic to practitioners. To name just two examples, selecting public servants with high PSM or offering training programmes to strengthen perceptions of a supportive work environment does, quite obviously, seem to be desirable. In and of itself, however, these 'lessons for practice' are not actionable. The crux is in *how* governments can select applicants with high PSM or train public servants to enhance their perception of a supportive work environment and, hence, intermittently boost their work motivation. Some recent work has moved towards providing such more actionable evidence and shown that effects are not as straightforward as generic recommendations assume (cf. Linos, 2018). Other works would do well to follow suit to provide practitioner-relevant evidence.

To ensure such evidence is not only actionable but also valid, public administration scholars would also do well to move towards greater methodological rigour. Two concerns stand out. First, the large number of factors affecting public sector work motivation (see Section 3) underscores that cross-sectional observational studies are suffering from a significant risk of omitted variable bias – and thus a risk of not providing valid insights. Yet, inferences in public administration scholarship are overwhelmingly based on this very research design. Moving towards longitudinal and experimental research designs is thus paramount – on top of qualitative works which can provide more granular evidence on how to enhance work motivation. Second, public administration scholars could make leaps by developing a universally accepted and validated measure of work motivation. Contrary to PSM and organizational commitment, no such measure exists; nor are most public administration works relying on creative objective measures used in other disciplines – such as fighter pilot victories. Instead, different public administration works measure work motivation through different (survey) measures, thwarting comparability. Scale development and validation is thus a priority for future research.

In sum, we hope this Element represents, most of all, a call for more holistic, actionable and methodologically rigorous public administration research on public sector work motivation. Public sector practitioners who seek to motivate public employees in times of austerity and future work tasks requiring ever greater self-motivation and commitment would stand to benefit.

Bibliography

Adams, J. S. (1965). Inequity In Social Exchange. *Advances in Experimental Social Psychology 2*, 267–99.

Ager, P., Bursztyn, L., & Voth, H.-J. (2016). *Killer Incentives: Status Competition and Pilot Performance during World War II*. (No. w22992). National Bureau of Economic Research.

Akerlof, G. A. (1984). *An Economic Theorist's Book of Tales*. Cambridge: Cambridge University Press.

Akerlof, G. A., & Kranton, R. E. (2000). Economics and Identity. *Quarterly Journal of Economics 115*(3), 715–53.

Allison, G. T. (1969). *Essence of Decision: Explaining the Cuban Missile Crisis*. London: Little Brown.

Andersen, L. B., Kristensen, N., & Pedersen, L. H. (2015). Documentation Requirements, Intrinsic Motivation, and Worker Absence. *International Public Management Journal 18*(4), 483–513.

Andersen, L. B., & Pallesen, T. (2008). Not Just for the Money? How Financial Incentives Affect the Number of Publications at Danish Research Institutions. *International Public Management Journal 11*, 28–47.

Andersen, L. B., Pedersen, L. H., & Petersen, O. H. (2018). Motivational Foundations of Public Service Provision: Towards a Theoretical Synthesis. *Perspectives on Public Management and Governance 1*(4), 283–98.

Andreoni, J. (1990). Impure Altruism and Donations to Public Goods: a Theory of Warm-Glow Giving. *Economic Journal 100*(401), 464–77.

Ashforth, B. E., & Mael, F. (1989). Social Identity Theory and the Organization. *The Academy of Management Review 14*(1), 20–39.

Ashikali, T., & Tanachia, S. (2015). Diversity Management in Public Organizations and Its Effect on Employees' Affective Commitment: the Role of Transformational Leadership and the Inclusiveness of the Organizational Culture. *Review of Public Personnel Administration 35*(2), 146–68.

Ashraf, N., Bandiera, O., & Jack, B. K. (2014). No Margin, No Mission? a Field Experiment on Incentives for Public Service Delivery. *Journal of Public Economics 120*(C), 1–17.

Ashraf, N., Bandiera, O., & Lee, S. S. (2014). Awards Unbundled: Evidence from a Natural Field Experiment. *Journal of Economic Behavior & Organization 100*(C), 44–63.

Baay, P. E., van Aken, M. A. G., van der Lippe, T., & de Ridder, D. T. D. (2014). Personality Moderates the Links of Social Identity with Work Motivation and Job Searching. *Frontiers in Psychology 5*, 1044.

Bandura, A. 1986. *Social Foundations of Thought and Action: a Social Cognitive Theory*. Englewood Cliffs, NJ: Prentice-Hall.

Barnard, C. I. (1968). *The Functions of the Executive*. Cambridge, MA: Harvard University Press.

Barr, A., & Serra, D. (2010). Corruption and Culture: an Experimental Analysis. *Journal of Public Economics 94*(11–12), 862–9.

Behn, R. D. (1995). The Big Questions of Public Management. *Public Administration Review, 55*(4), 313–24.

Bellé, N. (2013a). Experimental Evidence on the Relationship between Public Service Motivation and Job Performance. *Public Administration Review 73*(1), 143–53.

Bellé, N. (2013b). Leading to Make a Difference: a Field Experiment on the Performance Effects of Transformational Leadership, Perceived Social Impact, and Public Service Motivation. *Journal of Public Administration Research and Theory 24*(1), 109–36.

Bellé, N., & Cantarelli, P. (2015). Monetary Incentives, Motivation, and Job Effort in the Public Sector: an Experimental Study with Italian Government Executives. *Review of Public Personnel Administration 35* (2), 99–123.

Besley, T., & Ghatak, M. (2018). Prosocial Motivation and Incentives. *Annual Review of Economics 10*(1), 411–38.

Breaugh, J. A. (1985). The Measurement of Work Autonomy. *Human Relations 38*(6), 551–70.

Breaugh, J., Ritz, A., & Alfes, K. (2018). Work Motivation and Public Service Motivation: Disentangling Varieties of Motivation and Job Satisfaction. *Public Management Review 20*(10), 1423–43.

Brehm, J., & Gates, S. (1997). *Working, Shirking, and Sabotage*. Ann Arbor, MI: University of Michigan Press.

Brooks, G. R., & Wallace, J. P. (2006). A Discursive Examination of the Nature, Determinants and Impact of Organisational Commitment. *Asia Pacific Journal of Human Resources 44*(2), 222–39.

Bronkhorst, B., Steijn, B., & Vermeeren, B. (2015). Transformational Leadership, Goal Setting, and Work Motivation: the Case of a Dutch Municipality. *Review of Public Personnel Administration 35*(2), 124–45.

Bryson, A., & MacKerron, G. (2017). Are You Happy while You Work? *Economic Journal 127*(599), 106–25.

Buelens, M., & Van den Broeck, H. (2007). An Analysis of Differences in Work Motivation between Public and Private Sector Organizations. *Public Administration Review 67*(1), 65–74.

Burns, J. M. (1978). *Leadership*. New York: Harper & Row.

Caillier, J. G. (2013). Satisfaction with Work–Life Benefits and Organizational Commitment/Job Involvement: Is There a Connection? *Review of Public Personnel Administration 33*(4), 340–64.

Caillier, J. (2014). Do Role Clarity and Job Satisfaction Mediate the Relationship between Telework and Work Effort? *International Journal of Public Administration 37*(4): 193–201.

Carson, K. D., & Carson, P. P. (1997). Career Entrenchment: a Quiet March toward Occupational Death? *Academy of Management Executive 11*(1), 62–75.

Carton, A. M. (2018). 'I'm Not Mopping the Floors, I'm Putting a Man on the Moon': How NASA Leaders Enhanced the Meaningfulness of Work by Changing the Meaning of Work. *Administrative Science Quarterly 63*(2), 323–69.

Chatman, J. (1989). Improving Interactional Organizational Research: a Model of Person–Organization Fit. *Academy of Management Review 14*(3), 333–49.

Chan, H. F., Frey, B. S., Gallus, J., & Torgler, B. (2014). Academic Honors and Performance. *Labour Economics 31*, 188–204.

Chen, C. A., & Bozeman, B. (2013). Understanding Public and Nonprofit Managers' Motivation through the Lens of Self-Determination Theory. *Public Management Review 15*(4), 584–607.

Chen, C. M., Lee, P. C., & Chou, C. H. (2014). The Impact of Coproductive Taxpayers' Supervisory Behaviors on the Job Involvement of Tax Collectors. *Review of Public Personnel Administration 35*(3), 278–304.

Christensen, R. K., Paarlberg, L., & Perry, J. L. (2017). Public Service Motivation Research: Lessons for Practice. *Public Administration Review 77*(4), 529–42.

Clark, A. E (1997). Job Satisfaction and Gender: Why Are Women So Happy at Work? *Labour Economics 4*(4), 341–72.

Clark, P. B., & Wilson, J. Q. (1961). Incentive Systems: a Theory of Organizations. *Administrative Science Quarterly 6*(2), 129–66.

Cornelissen, J. P. (2012). Sensemaking under Pressure: The Influence of Professional Roles and Social Accountability on the Creation of Sense. *Organization Science 23*(1), 118–37.

Costa-Font, J., Jofre-Bonet, M., & Yen, S. T. (2013). Not All Incentives Wash Out the Warm Glow: the Case of Blood Donation Revisited. *Kyklos 66*(4), 529–51.

Crespi, L. P. (1942). Quantitative Variation of Incentive and Performance in the White Rat. *American Journal of Psychology 55*(4), 467–517.

Crewson, P. E. (1997). Public-Service Motivation: Building Empirical Evidence of Incidence and Effect. *Journal of Public Administration Research and Theory 7*(4), 499–518.

Cross, R., Rebele, R., & Grant, A. (2016, January–February). Collaborative Overload. *Harvard Business Review*, 57.

Csikszentmihalyi, M. (1975). *Beyond Boredom and Anxiety*. San Francisco: Jossey-Bass Publishers.

Dal Bó, E., Finan, F., & Rossi, M. A. (2013). Strengthening State Capabilities: the Role of Financial Incentives in the Call to Public Service. *Quarterly Journal of Economics 128*(3), 1169–1218.

Dawkins, R. (1989). *The Selfish Gene*. Oxford: Oxford University Press.

Damasio, A. R. (1994). *Descartes' Error: Emotion, Reason, and the Human Brain*. New York: Avon Books.

Deci, E. L., Eghrari, H., Patrick, B. C., & Leone, D. R. (1994). Facilitating Internalization: the Self-Determination Theory Perspective. *Journal of Personality 62*(1), 119–42.

Deci, E. L., Koestner, R., & Ryan, R. M. (1999). A Meta-analytic Review of Experiments Examining the Effects of Extrinsic Rewards on Intrinsic Motivation. *Psychological Bulletin* 125(6), 627–68; discussion 692–700.

Deci, E. L., & Ryan, R. M. (1985). *Intrinsic Motivation and Self-determination in Human Behavior*. New York: Springer.

DeHart-Davis L. (2009a). Green Tape: a Theory of Effective Organisational Rules. *Journal of Public Administration Research and Theory 19*(2), 361–84.

DeHart-Davis L. (2009b). Can Bureaucracy Benefit Organizational Women? an Exploratory Study. *Administration and Society 41*(3), 340–63.

DeHart-Davis, L., Davis, R. S., & Mohr, Z. (2015). Green Tape and Job Satisfaction: Can Organizational Rules Make Employees Happy? *Journal of Public Administration Research and Theory 25*(3), 849–76.

DeHart-Davis, L., Marlowe, J., & Pandey, S. K. (2006). Gender Dimensions of Public Service Motivation. *Public Administration Review 66*(6), 873–87.

Delfgaauw, J., & Dur, R. (2008). Incentives and Workers' Motivation in the Public Sector. *Economic Journal 118*(525), 171–91.

DiIulio, J. J. (2014). *Bring Back the Bureaucrats: Why More Federal Workers Will Lead to Better (and Smaller!) Government*. West Conshohocken, PA: Templeton Press.

Dilulio, J. D. (1994). Principled Agents: the Cultural Bases of Behavior in a Federal Government Bureaucracy. *Journal of Public Administration Research and Theory 4*(3), 277–318.

Dobrow, S., & Tosti-Kharas, J. (2011) Calling: The Development of a Scale Measure. *Personnel Psychology 64*(4), 1001–49

Duerst-Lahti, G., & Johnston, C. M. 1990. Gender and Style in Bureaucracy. *Women and Politics 10*(4), 67–120.

Dur, R., & Zoutenbier, R. (2015). Intrinsic Motivations of Public Sector Employees: Evidence for Germany. *German Economic Review 16*(3), 343–66.

Edmonson, A. (1999). Psychological Safety and Learning Behavior in Work Teams. *Administrative Science Quarterly 44*(2), 350–83.

Esteve, M., Schuster, C., Albareda, A., & Losada, C. (2017). The Effects of Doing More with Less in the Public Sector: Evidence from a Large-Scale Survey. *Public Administration Review 77*(4), 544–53.

Esteve, M., Urbig, D., van Witteloostuijn, A., & Boyne, G. (2016). Prosocial Behavior and Public Service Motivation. *Public Administration Review 76*(1), 177–87.

Fernandez, S., & Moldogaziev, T. T. (2013). Using Employee Empowerment to Encourage Innovative Behavior in the Public Sector. *Journal of Public Administration Research and Theory 23*(1), 155–87.

Frederickson, H. G. (1997). *The Spirit of Public Administration*. San Francisco: Jossey-Bass Publishers.

Frey, B. S., & Jegen, R. (2001). Motivation Crowding Theory. *Journal of Economic Surveys 15*(5), 589–611.

Frey, B. S., & Osterloh, M. (2002). Motivation: A Dual-Edged Factor of Production. In *Successful Management by Motivation*. Berlin, Heidelberg: Springer Berlin Heidelberg, 3–26.

Gallup. (2017). *State of the Global Workplace*. Washington, DC. www .gallup.com/workplace/238079/state-global-workplace-2017.aspx?utm_ source=link_wwwv9&utm_campaign=item_231668&utm_medium=copy (accessed 15 August 2018).

Graen, G. B., & Uhl-Bien, M. (1995). Relationship-Based Approach to Leadership: Development of Leader-Member Exchange (LMX) Theory of Leadership over 25 Years: Applying a Multi-level Multi-domain Perspective. *Leadership Quarterly 6* (2), 219–47.

Grant, A. M. (2008). Employees without a Cause: the Motivational Effects of Prosocial Impact in Public Service. *International Public Management Journal 11*(1), 48–66.

Grant, A. M. (2012). Leading with Meaning: Beneficiary Contact, Prosocial Impact, and the Performance Effects of Transformational Leadership. *Academy of Management Journal 55*(2), 458–76.

Grant, A. M., & Hofmann, D. A. (2011). It's Not All about Me: Motivating Hand Hygiene among Health Care Professionals by Focusing on Patients. *Psychological Science 22*(12), 1494–9.

Greenberg, J., & Baron, R. A. (2003). *Behavior in Organizations: Understanding and Managing the Human Side of Work.* Upper Saddle River, NJ: Prentice Hall.

Hackman, J. R. (1980). Work Redesign and Motivation. *Professional Psychology 11*(3), 445–55.

Herzberg, F. (1968). One More Time: How Do You Motivate Employees? *Harvard Business Review.*

Hill, C. A. (1987). Affiliation Motivation: People who Need People … but in Different Ways. *Journal of Personality and Social Psychology 52*(5), 1008–18.

Hood, C., James, O., Peters, G., & Scott, C. (2004). *Controlling Modern Government: Variety, Commonality, and Change.* Cheltenham: Edward Elgar.

Hsieh, J. Y. (2016). An Exploration of Antecedents and Simultaneity of Job Performance and Job Satisfaction across the Sectors. *Public Personnel Management 45*(1), 90–118.

Isen, A. M. (2000). Positive Affect and Decision Making. In M. Lewis & J. M. Haviland-Jones, eds., *Handbook of emotions*, 2nd ed. New York: Guilford Press, 417–35.

Jahan, F., & Shahan, A. M. (2012). Bureau Bashing and Public Service Motivation: A Case for the Civil Service of Bangladesh. *International Journal of Public Administration 35*(4), 272–84.

Jakobsen, M., & Jensen, R. (2015). Common Method Bias in Public Management Studies. *International Public Management Journal 18*(1), 3–30.

Kanfer, R. (1990). Motivation Theory and Industrial/Organizational Psychology. In M. D. Dunnette and L. Hough, eds., *Handbook of Industrial and Organizational Psychology, Volume 1: Theory in Industrial and Organisational Psychology.* Palo Alto, CA: Consulting Psychologist Press, 75–170.

Kanfer, R., & Ackerman, P. L. (2004). Aging, Adult Development, and Work Motivation. *Academy of Management Review 29*(3), 440–58.

Kaufman, H. (2006). *The Forest Ranger: A Study in Administrative Behavior.* Washington, DC: Resources for the Future.

Kellough, L., & Lu, H. (1993). The Paradox of Merit Pay in the Public Sector: Persistence of a Problematic Procedure. *Review of Public Personnel Administration 13*: 45–64.

Kim, S., & Rubianty, D. (2011). Perceived Fairness of Performance Appraisals in the Federal Government: Does It Matter? *Review of Public Personnel Administration 31*(4), 329–48.

Kim, S., & Vandenabeele, W. (2010). A Strategy for Building Public Service Motivation Research Internationally. *Public Administration Review 70*(5), 701–9.

Kim, S., Vandenabeele, W., Wright, B. E., Andersen, L. B., Cerase, F. P., Christensen, R. K., … & Palidauskaite, J. (2012). Investigating the Structure and Meaning of Public Service Motivation across Populations: Developing an International Instrument and Addressing Issues of Measurement Invariance. *Journal of Public Administration Research and Theory 23*(1), 79–102.

Kleinginna, P. R., & Kleinginna, A. M. (1981). A Categorized List of Motivation Definitions, with a Suggestion for a Consensual Definition. *Motivation and Emotion 5*(3), 263–91.

Knowles, E. (2014). *Oxford Dictionary of Quotations.* Oxford: Oxford University Press.

Kosfeld, M., & Neckermann, S. (2011). Getting More Work for Nothing? Symbolic Awards and Worker Performance. *American Economic Journal: Microeconomics 3*(3), 86–99.

Kramer, R. (1991). Cadenza Contra Text: Mozart in Beethoven's Hands. *19th-Century Music 15*(2), 116–31.

Landy, F. J., & Conte, J. M. (2010). *Work in the 21st Century: an Introduction to Industrial and Organizational Psychology.* Hoboken, NJ: Wiley-Blackwell.

Latham, G. P. (2012). *Work Motivation: History, Theory, Research, and Practice.* Thousand Oaks, CA: Sage.

Le Grand, J. (2003). *Motivation, Agency, and Public Policy.* Oxford: Oxford University Press.

Linos, E. (2018). More Than Public Service: a Field Experiment on Job Advertisements and Diversity in the Police. *Journal of Public Administration Research and Theory 28*(1), 67–85.

Locke, E. A., & Latham G. P. (2002). Building a Practically Useful Theory of Goal Setting and Task Motivation. *American Psychologist 57*(9), 705–17.

March, J. G. (1999). *The Pursuit of Organizational Intelligence.* Walden, MA: Blackwell Business.

March, J. G., & Simon, H. A. (1958). *Organizations.* New York: Wiley.

Marvel, J. D., & Resh, W. D. (2018). An Unconscious Drive to Help Others? Using the Implicit Association Test to Measure Prosocial Motivation. *International Public Management Journal 22*(1), 29–70.

Maslow, A. (1954). *Motivation and Personality.* New York: Harper.

80 Bibliography

McKinsey. (2017). *What the Future of Work Will Mean for Jobs, Skills, and Wages: Jobs Lost, Jobs Gained.* New York: McKinsey.

Medcof, J. W. (2006). Teamwork Goal Orientation as a New Component of Goal Orientation Conceptualization. *Academy of Management Proceedings* 1, 1–6.

Meyer-Sahling, J.-H., Schuster, C., & Mikkelsen, K. S. (2018). *Civil Service Management in Developing Countries: What Works? Evidence from a Survey with 23,000 Civil Servants in Africa, Asia, Eastern Europe and Latin America.* London: Report for the UK Department for International Development.

Meyer, J., & Allen, N. (1997). *Commitment in the Workplace: Theory, Research, and Application.* New York: Sage.

Meyer, J. P., Stanley, D. J., Herscovitch, L., & Topolnytsky, L. (2002). Affective, Continuance, and Normative Commitment to the Organization: A Meta-analysis of Antecedents, Correlates, and Consequences. *Journal of Vocational Behavior 61*(1), 20–52.

Miao, Q., Newman, A., Schwarz, G., & Xu, Lin. 2014. Servant Leadership, Trust, and the Organizational Commitment of Public Sector Employees in China. *Public Administration 92*(3), 727–43.

Mitchell, T. R. (1982). Motivation: New Directions for Theory, Research, and Practice. *The Academy of Management Review 7*(1), 80.

Mitchell, T. R., & Daniels, D. 2003. Motivation. In W. C. Borman, D. R. Ilgen, & R. J. Klimoski, eds., *Comprehensive Handbook of Psychology: Industrial and Organizational Psychology.* New York: Wiley, 225–54.

Moldogaziev, T. T. & Silva C. (2015). Fostering Affective Organizational Commitment in Public Sector Agencies: the Significance of Multifaceted Leadership Roles. *Public Administration 93*(3), 557–75.

Moore, M. H. (1996). *Creating Public Value: Strategic Management in Government.* Cambridge, MA: Harvard University Press.

Moynihan, D., & Pandey, S. (2007). Finding Workable Levers over Work Motivation: Comparing Job Satisfaction, Job Involvement, and Organizational Commitment. *Administration and Society 39*(7), 803–32.

Neumann, O., & Ritz, A. (2015). Public Service Motivation and Rational Choice Modelling. *Public Money & Management 35*(5), 365–70.

Niskanen, W. (1968). The Peculiar Economics of Bureaucracy. *American Economic Review 58*(2), 293–305.

OECD. (2005). *Performance-Related Pay Policies for Government Employees.* Paris: OECD.

OECD. (2016). *Engaging Public Employees for a High-Performing Civil Service.* Paris: OECD.

Osborne, D. (1993). Reinventing Government. *Public Productivity & Management Review 16*(4), 349.

Ospina S., Esteve M., & Seulki L. (2018). Assessing Qualitative Studies in Public Management Research. *Public Administration Review 78*(4), 593–605.

Osterloh, M., & Frey, B. S. (2013). Motivation Governance. In *Handbook of Economic Organization*. Cheltenham: Edward Elgar Publishing.

Paarlberg, L. (2007). The Impact of Customer Orientation on Government Employee Performance. *International Public Management Journal 10*(2), 201–31.

Paarlberg, L. E., & Lavigna, B. (2010). Transformational Leadership and Public Service Motivation: Driving Individual and Organizational Performance. *Public Administration Review 70*(5), 710–18.

Pandey, S. K., & Stazyk, E. C. (2008). Antecedents and Correlates of Public Service Motivation. In J. L. Perry & A. Hondeghem, eds., *Motivation in Public Management: the Call of Public Service*. Oxford: Oxford University Press, 101–17.

Pavey, L., Greitemeyer, T., & Sparks, P. (2012). 'I Help Because I Want to, Not Because You Tell Me to'. *Personality and Social Psychology Bulletin 38*(5), 681–9.

Perry, James, Engbers, Trent, & Yun Jun, So (2009). Back to the Future? Performance-Related Pay, Empirical Research, and the Perils of Persistence. *Public Administration Review 69*(1), 39–51.

Perry, J. L. (1996). Measuring Public Service Motivation: an Assessment of Construct Reliability and Validity. *Journal of Public Administration Research and Theory 6*(1), 5–22.

Perry, J. L. (1997). Antecedents of Public Service Motivation. *Journal of Public Administration Research and Theory 7*(2), 181–97.

Perry, J. L., Brudney, J. L., Coursey, D., & Littlepage, L. (2008). What Drives Morally Committed Citizens? A Study of the Antecedents of Public Service Motivation. *Public Administration Review 68*(3), 445–58.

Perry, J. L., & Hondeghem, A. (2008). *Motivation in Public Management: the Call of Public Service*. Oxford: Oxford University Press.

Perry, J. L., Hondeghem, A., & Wise, L. R. (2010). Revisiting the Motivational Bases of Public Service: Twenty Years of Research and an Agenda for the Future. *Public Administration Review 70*(5), 681–90.

Perry, J. L., Mesch, D., & Paarlberg, L. (2006). Motivating Employees in a New Governance Era: the Performance Paradigm Revisited. *Public Administration Review 66*(4), 505–14.

Perry, J. L., & Porter, L. W. (1982). Factors Affecting the Context for Motivation in Public Organizations. *Academy of Management Review 7*(1), 89–98.

Perry, J. L., & Rainey, H. G. (1988). The Public-Private Distinction in Organization Theory: a Critique and Research Strategy. *Academy of Management Review 13*(2), 182–201.

Perry, J. L., & Wise, L. R. (1990). The Motivational Bases of Public Service. *Public Administration Review 50*(3), 367–73.

Petter, J., Byrnes, P., Choi, D., Fegan, F., & Miller, R. (2002). Dimensions and Patterns in Employee Empowerment: Assessing What Matters to Street-Level Bureaucrats. *Journal of Public Administration Research and Theory* 12(3), 377–400.

Pinder, C. C. (2008). *Work Motivation in Organizational Behavior.* New York: Psychology Press.

Pink, D. H. (2009). *Drive: the Surprising Truth about What Motivates Us.* New York: Riverhead Books.

Pitts, D. (2009). Diversity Management, Job Satisfaction, and Performance: Evidence from U.S. Federal Agencies. *Public Administration Review 69*(2), 328–38.

Porter, L. W., Steers, R. M., Mowday, R. T., & Boulian, P. V. (1974). Organizational Commitment, Job Satisfaction, and Turnover among Psychiatric Technicians. *Journal of Applied Psychology 59*(5), 603–9.

Posner, B. Z., & Schmidt, W. H. (1996). The Values of Business and Federal Government Executives: More Different than Alike. *Personnel Administration 25*(3), 277–89.

Prebble, M. (2016). Has the Study of Public Service Motivation Addressed the Issues that Motivated the Study? *American Review of Public Administration 46*(3), 267–91.

Rainey, H. G. (2014). *Understanding and Managing Public Organizations.* New York: John Wiley & Sons.

Rainey, H. G., & Steinbauer, P. (1999). Galloping Elephants: Developing Elements of a Theory of Effective Government Organizations. *Journal of Public Administration Research and Theory 9*(1), 1–32.

Resh, W. G., Marvel, J. D., & Wen, B. (2018). The Persistence of Prosocial Work Effort as a Function of Mission Match. *Public Administration Review 78*(1), 116–25.

Ritz, A., Brewer, G. A., & Neumann, O. (2016). Public Service Motivation: a Systematic Literature Review and Outlook. *Public Administration Review 76*(3), 414–26.

Ryan, R. M., & Deci, E. L. (2000a). Intrinsic and Extrinsic Motivations: Classic Definitions and New Directions. *Contemporary Educational Psychology 25*(1), 54–67.

Ryan, R. M., & Deci, E. L. (2000b). Self-Determination Theory and the Facilitation of Intrinsic Motivation, Social Development, and Well-Being Self-Determination Theory. *American Psychologist 55*(1), 68–78.

Sabharwal, M. (2014). Is Diversity Management Sufficient? Organizational Inclusion to Further Performance. *Public Personnel Management* 43(2), 197–217.

Schaef, A. W., & Fassel, D. (1988). *The Addictive Organization*. San Francisco: Harper & Row.

Seo, M.G., Barret, L. F., & Bartunek, J. M. (2004). The Role of Affective Experience in Work Motivation. *Academy of Management Review 29*(3), 423–39.

Shepsle, K. (2010) *Analyzing Politics: Rationality, Behavior, and Institutions.* New York: W. W. Norton & Company

Sinek, S. (2017). *Leaders Eat Last: Why Some Teams Pull Together and Others Don't*. New York: Random House.

Skinner, B. F., & Burrhus F. (1953). *Science and Human Behavior.* London: Macmillan.

Stazyk, E. C., Pandey, S., & Wright, B. E. (2011). Understanding Affective Organizational Commitment: the Importance of Institutional Context. *American Review of Public Administration 41*(6), 603–24.

Tendler, J., & Freedheim, S. (1994). Trust in a Rent-Seeking World: Health and Government Transformed in Northeast Brazil. *World Development 22*(12), 1771–91.

The Guardian. (2009). Case study: Fighting bureaucracy in the police force. www.theguardian.com/society/2009/sep/30/fighting-bureaucracy-police-force (accessed 5 November 2018).

The Guardian. (2010). Lazy Bureaucrats, Burden or Blessing? www.theguardian.com/education/2010/feb/09/improbable-research-lazy-bureaucrats (accessed 27 August 2018).

The Independent. (2013). The Graphene Story: How Andrei Geim and Kostya Novoselov Hit on a Scientific Breakthrough that Changed the World … by Playing with Sticky Tape. www.independent.co.uk/news/science/the-graphene-story-how-andrei-geim-and-kostya-novoselov-hit-on-a-scientific-breakthrough-that-8539743.html (accessed 4 November 2018).

The Telegraph. (2010). Third of police time 'is wasted on bureaucracy'. www.telegraph.co.uk/news/uknews/law-and-order/8069928/Third-of-police-time-is-wasted-on-bureaucracy.html (accessed 5 November 2018).

The Telegraph. (2012). How Pep Guardiola Got the Barcelona Players on His Side to Halt Team's Decline into Decadence. www.telegraph.co.uk/sport/ football/teams/barcelona/9683924/How-Pep-Guardiola-got-the-Barcelona-players-on-his-side-to-halt-teams-decline-into-decadence.html (accessed 4 November 2018).

The Telegraph. (2015). How Beethoven Redesigned the Cadenza – Twice. www .telegraph.co.uk/music/artists/how-beethoven-redesigned-the-cadenza–twice/ (accessed 3 November 2018).

Thomas, K. W. (2000). *Intrinsic motivation at Work: Building Energy & Commitment.* Oakland, CA: Berrett-Koehler Publishers.

Ting, Y. (1997). Determinants of Job Satisfaction of Federal Government Employees. *Personnel Administration 26*(3), 313–34.

Tummers, L. G., & Knies, E. (2013). Leadership and Meaningful Work in the Public Sector. *Public Administration Review 73*(6), 859–68.

Vandenabeele, W. (2007). Toward a Public Administration Theory of Public Service Motivation. *Public Management Review 9*(4), 545–56.

Van Loon, N. (2017). From Red Tape to Which Performance Results? Exploring the Relationship between Red Tape and Various Dimensions of Performance in Healthcare Work Units. *Public Administration 95*(1), 60–77.

van Loon, N. M., Vandenabeele, W., & Leisink, P. (2015). On the Bright and Dark Side of Public Service Motivation: the Relationship between PSM and Employee Wellbeing. *Public Money & Management 35*(5), 349–56.

Vigoda, E. (2000). Organizational Politics, Job Attitudes, and Work Outcomes: Exploration and Implications for the Public Sector. *Journal of Vocational Behavior 57*(3), 326–347.

Vroom, V. H. (1964). *Work and Motivation.* New York: Wiley.

Warr, P. (2001). Age and Work Behavior: Physical Attributes, Cognitive Abilities, Knowledge, Personality Traits, and Motives. *International Review of Industrial and Organizational Psychology 16*, 1–36.

Weber, M. (1978). *Economy and Society: an Outline of Interpretive Sociology.* Berkeley: University of California Press.

Wegener, D. T., & Petty, R. E. (1996). Effects of Mood on Persuasion Processes: Enhancing, Reducing, and Biasing Scrutiny of Attitude-Relevant Information. In L. L. Martin & A. Tesser, eds., *Striving and feeling: Interactions among goals, affect, and self-regulation.* Mahwah, NJ: Lawrence Erlbaum Associates, 329–62.

Wiener, Y. (1982). Commitment in Organizations: a Normative View. *Academy of Management Review 7*(3), 418–28.

Wildman, J., & Hollingsworth, B. (2009). Blood Donation and the Nature of Altruism. *Journal of Health Economics 28*(2), 492–503.

Wilson, J. Q. (1978). *The Investigators: Managing FBI and Narcotics Agents*. New York: Basic Books.

Wilson, J. Q. (1989). *Bureaucracy: What Government Agencies Do and Why They Do It*. New York: Basic Books.

World Bank. (2016). *How Shanghai Does It: Insights and Lessons from the Highest-Ranking Education System in the World*. Washington, DC.

Wright, B. E. (2001). Public-Sector Work Motivation: a Review of the Current Literature and a Revised Conceptual Model. *Journal of Public Administration Research and Theory 11*(4), 559–86.

Wright, B. E. (2004). The Role of Work Context in Work Motivation: a Public Sector Application of Goal and Social Cognitive Theories. *Journal of Public Administration Research and Theory 14*(1), 59–78.

Wright, B. E. & Pandey, S. (2008). Public Service Motivation and the Assumption of Person-Organization Fit: Testing the Mediating Effect of Value Congruence. *Administration & Society 40*(5), 502–21.

Cambridge Elements ☰

Public and Nonprofit Administration

Andrew Whitford
University of Georgia

Andrew Whitford is Alexander M. Crenshaw Professor of Public Policy in the School of Public and International Affairs at the University of Georgia. His research centers on strategy and innovation in public policy and organization studies.

Robert Christensen
Brigham Young University

Robert Christensen specializes in nonprofit and public management. He is Division Chair for the Public and Nonprofit Division at the Academy of Management and serves as an elected member of the Public Management Research Association board.

About the Series
The foundation of this series are cutting-edge contributions on emerging topics and definitive reviews of keystone topics in public and nonprofit administration, especially those that lack longer treatment in textbook or other formats. Among keystone topics of interest for scholars and practitioners of public and nonprofit administration, it covers public management, public budgeting and finance, nonprofit studies, and the interstitial space between the public and nonprofit sectors, along with theoretical and methodological contributions, including quantitative, qualitative and mixed-methods pieces.

The Public Management Research Association
The Public Management Research Association improves public governance by advancing research on public organizations, strengthening links among interdisciplinary scholars, and furthering professional and academic opportunities in public management.

Cambridge Elements ≡

Public and Nonprofit Administration

Elements in the Series

Printed in the United States
By Bookmasters